THE DRIVING TEST

PASS

FIRST TIME

THEORY

By
Dr. Michael C. Cox

AA Publishing

Produced by AA Publishing in association with The Associated Examining Board and the National Extension College.

© The Automobile Association 1996
First published 1996.

Crown copyright material reproduced under licence from the Controller of HMSO and the Driving Standards Agency.

ISBN 0 7495 1408 6

Published by AA Publishing (a trading name of Automobile Association Developments Limited, whose registered office is Norfolk House, Priestley Road, Basingstoke, Hampshire RG24 9NY; registered number 1878835).

The contents of this book are believed correct at the time of printing. Nevertheless, the publishers cannot be held responsible for any errors or omissions or for changes in the details given in this book or for the consequences of any reliance on the information provided by the same.

Colour separation by Anton Graphics, Andover
Printed by Graficromo S.A., Spain

From July 1996 learner drivers must pass a theory test and a practical test to get a full driving licence.

YOUR QUESTIONS ANSWERED

Q. *Why a theory test?*
A. To check that drivers know and understand what to do before they do it.

Q. *How will it work?*
A. The test will be 30 multiple-choice questions.

Q. *What is a multiple-choice question?*
A. One with 4, 5 or 6 answers to choose from.

Q. *What will the test cover?*
A. All the topics listed in this book.

ABOUT THIS BOOK

This book will help you to pass your theory test.

- it explains and revises the theory of driving
- it has lots of useful advice and information
- it has all the official questions and answers

The book is divided into four main sections. The questions are arranged under the fifteen official syllabus topics. Questions dealing with related aspects of a topic are grouped together. Notes and explanations follow each question or group of questions. All the correct answers are at the back of the book.

HOW TO USE THIS BOOK

1. Look at the list of topics on page 4 and turn to one you find interesting.
2. Read the first question and tick your choice of answer(s).
3. Study any note or explanation following the question.
4. Check your answer(s) against the correct answers at the back of the book.
5. Make sure you understand the answers before you try the next question.

> If you understand and learn your driving theory you should **pass** the test and be a better driver

WARNING

Do **not** try too many questions at once.
Do **not** try to learn the answers by heart.
The order of the answers in this book may be different from how they are arranged in the actual test – so do **not** try to memorise the order.

You now have to pass two driving tests before you can apply for a full driving licence. The new test, introduced in July 1996, is a written theory test, and this book contains all the **real questions** that you may have to answer.

PREPARING FOR BOTH TESTS

You are strongly recommended to prepare for the theory test at the same time as you develop your skills behind the wheel. Obviously, there are many similarities between the two tests – it is all about helping to make you a safer driver on today's busy roads. By preparing for both tests at the same time, you will reinforce your knowledge and understanding of all aspects of driving and you will improve your chances of passing both tests first time.

THE THEORY TEST

At the time of printing, the pass mark for the theory test is 26 out of the 35 questions. You will have 40 minutes to complete the paper and all questions are multiple-choice. The Government may change the pass mark from time to time. Your driving school will be able to tell you if there has been a change. Also, the Government may, from time to time, introduce new or amended questions. However, if you are fully prepared on each topic, you will be in a position to answer any question.

SELECTING A DRIVING SCHOOL

When you select a driving school to teach you the practical skills, make sure they are prepared to advise and help you with the theory test. Check with friends who have been taught recently and make sure you understand the difference between an instructor who displays a pink badge (a trainee instructor) and one who displays a green badge (a fully qualified instructor). Price is important, so find out whether the school offers any discounts for blocks or courses of lessons paid in advance; if you decide to pay in advance, make sure the driving school is reputable. If lesson prices are very low, ask yourself 'why?' And don't forget to ask about the car you'll be learning to drive in. Is it modern and reliable? Is it insured?

WHAT TO EXPECT

As with all courses, there are a number of subjects you will need to master. All good driving schools will have available a progress sheet and syllabus which sets out all the skills you will need and keeps a record of your progress. You will probably find that if you take a two-hour lesson every week, your rate of progress will surprise you!

It is important to book and take your theory test at an early stage in your course of practical lessons. After 31 December 1996 you will have to pass the theory test before you can apply for the practical test.

After a few hours of tuition the instructor will discuss with you a structured course to suit your needs and you can agree on the likely date when you will be ready to take the practical test. You can then apply for a practical test appointment; this will give you added incentive to prepare thoroughly.

THE AA'S DRIVING SCHOOL

The AA has a driving school staffed by fully qualified instructors, who are all familiar with this book, the theory test and the practical test. Why not give them a try? You can ring for details on freephone **0800 60 70 80.**

KNOWLEDGE, SKILLS AND ATTITUDE

Being a good driver is more than just having the knowledge and the skills – it is about applying them with the right attitude. No one is a 'natural' or a 'perfect driver'. All drivers make mistakes. Being careful, courteous and considerate to other road users will complement the skills and knowledge you will acquire in the coming weeks and make you a good driver.

Preface by **Linda Hatswell and Nick Bravery** – AA The Driving School

HOW TO ANSWER THE QUESTIONS

Each question has four, five or six answers. You must mark the boxes with the correct answers. Each question tells you how many answers to mark. Study each question carefully. Sometimes you can find the correct answers by rejecting the incorrect answers.

1 Read all the words.
2 Look at any diagram, drawing or photograph.
3 Make sure you understand the question
4 If in doubt, go through the question again.

A RANGE OF PRODUCTS TO HELP YOU

The Associated Examining Board, The National Extension College and the AA have joined together to produce a range of teaching and learning products: The Theory Test on Disk (AA), The Theory Test Open Learning Pack (NEC) and the Theory Test Classroom Pack (AEB). You can get information about these products from:

The Associated Examining Board, Development Office, Stag Hill House, Guildford, Surrey. GU2 5XJ

The four topics in this section are about **you**. The first two are about your abilities as a driver. The last two are about other road users and your attitude towards them.

ALERTNESS

Good drivers are **alert**. This means you must stay wide awake and on the lookout for danger. You must *concentrate* on your driving. You must *observe* and *be aware* of what is happening all around to *anticipate* the actions of other road users and deal with any danger – hidden or in view. You cannot afford to become bored or distracted. Lose your concentration and you could lose your life!

HAZARD AWARENESS

Good drivers are **perceptive**. They see and hear danger. Sometimes they may even feel and smell it. To be a perceptive driver you must do more than just look and listen. You must constantly *scan* the road well ahead. You must *process* all the *information* you see and hear in order to *detect*, *identify* and *interpret* all the hazards.

> **Always pay attention and give yourself as much time as possible to decide what to do**

As well as being alert, perceptive and quick to detect, identify and interpret hazards, good drivers are also skilled at **judging** and **deciding** what to do. They always adjust their position and speed to gain time for dealing with any hazard in the best way. For hazards involving other road users, good drivers will judge and decide when to speed up, move forward and take priority and when to slow down, hold back and give priority.

> **You must learn good judgement and decision taking**

Colour blindness or deafness should not prevent you from passing your test but could make driving more difficult and hazardous. If you need spectacles or contact lenses, you must wear them. It is an offence to drive with uncorrected eyesight. Impairment is anything that reduces or weakens our abilities and senses. Our sight, hearing and other abilities often become impaired as we get older. That is why drivers must renew their licence at age 70 and sign a declaration of their fitness when they renew their licence every three years after that.

Ill-health, drugs and medication can impair your driving. Anyone suffering from daytime epilepsy is not allowed even a provisional driving licence. If you are diabetic you should avoid driving if you have not eaten for two hours.

Stress and tiredness can also impair your driving. Falling asleep at the wheel is a common but avoidable cause of accidents.

Do not drive if you are tired

Alcohol, even in very small amounts, can seriously affect your driving. The legal limits of alcohol are 35 micrograms per 100 ml of breath, 80 milligrams per 100 ml of blood and 107 milligrams per 100 ml of urine. It is an offence to refuse to give a specimen for an alcohol test. You will lose your licence if you are over the limit when driving or just in charge of a motor vehicle. And you can still be charged with a drink driving offence even if you are below the legal limit.

NEVER DRINK AND DRIVE

VULNERABLE ROAD USERS

People cause 95% of all road accidents. Other road users are people. To someone else **you** are the other road user. And you could be a pedestrian, cyclist, moped rider, motorcyclist or motorist. Pedestrians are very vulnerable road users, especially when they are elderly or disabled people with slow reactions or when they are young children with quick unpredictable reactions. You may not always see them: a pedestrian in a dark coat is not very conspicuous at night. The same is true of a cyclist without lights!

You must watch out for cyclists, especially younger ones. They may suddenly veer sideways and they are easily blown off course by wind and rain. Moped riders and motorcyclists are less affected by weather but they can be as vulnerable as cyclists. Buses, coaches, large vehicles and articulated lorries present their drivers with different problems. They need time to speed up or slow down, and room to manoeuvre. Remember that passengers stepping from a bus or coach could become pedestrians on the road ahead of you.

ATTITUDE

To be a good driver, you must be **courteous** and **considerate** towards other road users. You must recognise the value of eye contact. You must be aware of the risks to pedestrians and cyclists. You should keep safe distances from other vehicles and give priority where appropriate. You should realise that some road users, like the newly qualified licence holder, will lack experience. Some drivers, like the elderly and the disabled, may be at a disadvantage. They may rely on you for their safety.

Careless and inconsiderate driving is a serious offence carrying a maximum fine of £2500 and a risk of disqualification

Q1 **To move off safely from a parked position you should**

Mark one answer

○ **A.** Give a hand signal as well as using your indicators

○ **B.** NOT look round if there is a parked vehicle close in front of you

○ **C.** Signal if other drivers will need to slow down

○ **D.** Use your mirrors and look round for a final check

Q2 **You want to move off from a parked position. The road is busy with traffic passing from behind. You should**

Mark one answer

○ **A.** Signal while waiting for a gap in the traffic

○ **B.** Wait without signalling for a safe gap in the traffic

○ **C.** Edge your way into the traffic until someone gives way

○ **D.** Give a signal and move away as soon as someone flashes you

Your signal shows what you intend to do. So you must signal correctly at the right time. Before you signal, make sure it is safe to do whatever you intend. For example, only when there is a safe gap in the traffic should you signal your intention to move off. Your signal to other traffic is a warning **not** an order. You **cannot** tell other road users what to do.

Q3 **What is the safest way to brake?**

Mark one answer

○ **A.** Put your gear lever into neutral, brake hard then ease off just before stopping

○ **B.** Brake hard, put your gear lever into neutral and pull your handbrake on just before stopping

○ **C.** Brake lightly, then harder as you begin to stop then ease off just before stopping

○ **D.** Brake lightly, push your clutch pedal down and pull your handbrake on just before stopping

Never brake hard except in a real emergency. Always use 'progressive' braking. Keep in gear for as long as possible. When the car has stopped, use the handbrake to set (lock on) the rear brakes.

Q4 **You are reversing into a side road. Whilst reversing you should look mainly**

Mark one answer
- ⬭ **A.** Into the interior mirror
- ⬭ **B.** Through the rear window
- ⬭ **C.** Into the door mirror nearest the kerb
- ⬭ **D.** Into the door mirror away from the kerb

Look where you are going. When going forwards driving normally, this means looking through your front window most of the time. When going backwards driving in reverse, this means looking through your rear window most of the time.

Q5 **When turning your car in the road, you should**

Mark one answer
- ⬭ **A.** Overhang the kerb
- ⬭ **B.** Use a driveway if possible
- ⬭ **C.** Check all around for other road users
- ⬭ **D.** Keep your hand on the handbrake throughout

Whatever you are doing, you must be alert and show consideration for other road users. You should choose a safe and convenient place if you need to turn in the road. Do not put pedestrians in danger. Do not inconvenience other road users.

Q6 **In which situation should you expect other vehicles to overtake you on either side?**

Mark one answer
- ⬭ **A.** In a one-way street
- ⬭ **B.** In a contraflow
- ⬭ **C.** On a dual carriageway
- ⬭ **D.** On a motorway

The rule is: overtake on the right. But here are two exceptions. The traffic is moving slowly in queues and the right queue is moving more slowly than the left queue. A vehicle which is going to turn left at the end of a one-way street is allowed to pass a slower vehicle which is going to turn right at the end of the one-way street. See **Q131, Q307.**

Q7 **You are driving at night and are dazzled by the headlights of an oncoming car. You should**

Mark one answer
- A. Close your eyes
- B. Flash your headlights
- C. Pull down the sun visor
- D. Slow down or stop

Keep your eyes open and on the road. Try to avoid looking directly at oncoming headlights. Do not dazzle other road users: dip your headlights in good time. See **Q142, Q145–148.**

Q8 **You are driving a vehicle fitted with a hand telephone. To answer the telephone you MUST**

Mark one answer
- A. Be particularly careful at junctions
- B. Find a safe place to stop
- C. Reduce your speed
- D. Steer the car with one hand

Q9 **You should ONLY use a hand-held telephone**

Mark one answer
- A. If you need to make an emergency call
- B. If your vehicle has an automatic gear change
- C. When you are travelling on a minor road
- D. When you have stopped at a safe place

You must stop to use a **hand-held** telephone. You may stop on the hard shoulder of a motorway **but** in a real emergency only. You cannot pay proper attention to your driving if you are using any telephone.

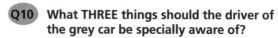

Q10 **What THREE things should the driver of the grey car be specially aware of?**

Mark three answers
- ◯ **A.** Cars leaving parking spaces
- ◯ **B.** Empty parking spaces
- ◯ **C.** Other cars behind the grey car
- ◯ **D.** Parked cars' doors opening
- ◯ **E.** Pedestrians stepping out between cars
- ◯ **F.** The bumpy road surface

Q11 **What are TWO main hazards a driver should be aware of when driving along this street?**

Mark two answers
- ◯ **A.** Car doors opening suddenly
- ◯ **B.** Children running out from between vehicles
- ◯ **C.** Glare from the sun
- ◯ **D.** Lack of road markings
- ◯ **E.** Large goods vehicles
- ◯ **F.** The headlights on parked cars being switched on

Always look ahead. Watch out for *pedestrians*, especially children, the elderly and the disabled. They can appear from nowhere and step into your path without warning. You must also watch for other *moving* hazards such as car doors suddenly opening and vehicles moving off without any indication. You must also keep an eye on vehicles following behind you and make sure you do not put them in any danger by acting unpredictably. See **Q304**.

Q12 **What should the driver of the red car do?**

Mark one answer
- ◯ **A.** Quickly drive behind the pedestrian in the road
- ◯ **B.** Tell the pedestrian in the road she should not have crossed
- ◯ **C.** Wait for the pedestrian in the road to cross
- ◯ **D.** Wave on the pedestrians who are waiting to cross

You must always give priority to pedestrians *in danger on the road*. Remember how vulnerable they are. If you are stopping for pedestrians to cross, signal properly your intentions to other road users. Make eye contact with the pedestrians but do not wave them across. You have no authority to tell others what to do. You can only tell others what **you** intend to do.

Q13 **What should the driver of the white car do?**

Mark one answer
- ⬭ **A.** Drive on slowly
- ⬭ **B.** Stop and let the pedestrian cross
- ⬭ **C.** Stop only if there is a car behind
- ⬭ **D.** Wave the pedestrian to go back

You must never put pedestrians in danger by failing to give them priority. However, pedestrians should not expect always to be given priority. Drive carefully with courtesy and consideration for others.

Q14 **What should the driver of the car approaching the crossing do?**

Mark one answer
- ⬭ **A.** Continue at the same speed
- ⬭ **B.** Drive through quickly
- ⬭ **C.** Slow and get ready to stop
- ⬭ **D.** Sound the horn

Approach crossings with care especially when pedestrians are waiting or seem about to step into the road. Be prepared to slow down. Remember to use your mirror and signal your intentions to other road users. Make eye contact with the pedestrians and give a proper arm signal. Do not wave them on to the crossing. See **Q102, Q103, Q430, Q431.**

Q15 **What should the cars on the pelican crossing have done?**

Mark one answer
- ⬭ **A.** Got closer to the cars in front
- ⬭ **B.** Left a space in the queue of traffic
- ⬭ **C.** Put their hazard warning lights on
- ⬭ **D.** Waited before the zigzag lines

Pedestrian crossings are areas of road where pedestrians have absolute priority. Never block a crossing by driving on to it if your way forward is not clear. You may stop in front or behind the crossing within the area marked by zigzag lines on the road to give precedence to pedestrians or to obey the crossing signals. See **Q314, Q431.**

Q16 Which road user has caused a hazard?

Mark one answer
- A. The car turning (arrowed D)
- B. The moving car (arrowed C)
- C. The parked car (arrowed A)
- D. The pedestrian waiting to cross (arrowed B)

It is normally an offence to stop within the area marked by zigzag lines because it increases the dangers to pedestrians using the crossing by obstructing the view of other road users. You **must not** **stop** in that area even to pick up or set down a disabled passenger.

Q17 What is the main hazard shown in this picture?

Mark one answer
- A. The cyclist crossing the road
- B. Parked cars around the corner
- C. Vehicles doing U-turns
- D. Vehicles turning right

Always watch for the road user doing the unexpected. On dual carriageways right turns may be allowed but not U-turns and parking. Cyclists may be allowed to use the dual the carriageway but not to cross the lanes in the path of oncoming traffic as seems likely here. Crossing at the traffic lights would be much safer.

Q18 What is the main hazard a driver should be aware of when following this cyclist?

Mark one answer
- A. The contents of the cyclist's carrier may fall on to the road
- B. The cyclist may move in to the left and dismount
- C. The cyclist may swerve out into the road
- D. The cyclist may wish to turn right at the end of the road

Always be prepared for a cyclist to change direction without warning. Be patient and hold back until you can overtake safely. Keep enough distance between you and the cyclist so that you can stop your vehicle in good time.

Q19 **The driver of which car has caused a hazard?**

Mark one answer
- **A.** Car A
- **B.** Car B
- **C.** Car C
- **D.** Car D

At a STOP sign you **must stop** (not behind or over but) **at** the solid **white line**. Car A has forced other cars to move on to the diagonal white lines hazard markings for the right-turn lane.

Q20 **What is the main hazard the driver of the red car (arrowed) should be most aware of?**

Mark one answer
- **A.** The black car may stop suddenly
- **B.** The bus may move out into the road
- **C.** Glare from the sun may affect the driver's vision
- **D.** Oncoming vehicles will assume the driver is turning right

Always look ahead for the possibility of buses and coaches pulling in or moving off. Remember that these large vehicles are often difficult to manoeuvre and their drivers have poorer vision behind them. The red car could well be in the bus driver's blind spot. See **Q67, Q124.**

Q21 **What should the driver of the red car (arrowed) do?**

Mark one answer
- **A.** Sound the horn to tell other drivers where he is
- **B.** Squeeze through the gap
- **C.** Wait until the car blocking the way has moved
- **D.** Wave the driver of the white car to go on

Drivers should be patient. The driver of the red car should, if possible, make eye contact with the other car drivers. It is then up to those drivers to decide when it is safe for them to move. The driver should sound the horn only if other moving vehicles pose a danger.

Q22 **What should the driver of the grey car (arrowed) do?**

Mark one answer
○ **A.** Cross if the way is clear
○ **B.** Reverse out of the box junction
○ **C.** Wait in the same place until the lights are green
○ **D.** Wait until the lights are red then cross

You may enter a yellow box junction if you want to turn right and are only prevented by oncoming vehicles or by others turning right. Otherwise, you *must not* enter until your exit road or lane from the box junction is clear. The same basic rule applies to all junctions: do not proceed unless your way forward is clear. **Q313.**

Q23 **What should you do when approaching a level crossing with lights flashing?**

Mark one answer
○ **A.** Drive through carefully
○ **B.** Drive through quickly
○ **C.** Stop before the barrier
○ **D.** Switch on hazard warning lights

A *steady* amber light always means stop. At railway crossings the steady amber light is usually followed immediately by two flashing red lights. You should keep going if you have already crossed the white line when the amber light comes on. But you *must not* cross the line when the red lights are flashing even if a train has gone by. It is only safe to cross when the lights go off and the barriers open.

Q24 **In heavy motorway traffic you are being followed closely by the vehicle behind. How can you lower the risk of an accident?**

Mark one answer
○ **A.** Increase your distance from the vehicle in front
○ **B.** Move on to the hard shoulder and stop
○ **C.** Switch on your hazard lights
○ **D.** Tap your foot on the brake pedal

You control the gap between you and the vehicle in front of yours. You cannot control the distance between you and the vehicle behind you. Always try to let dangerous drivers get in front of you where you can see them. Remember you are not in a race. Anyway, racing on the public highway is a serious offence in the eyes of the law.

Q25 **To drive legally you must be able to read a number plate from what distance?**

Mark one answer
- A. 10 metres (33 feet)
- B. 15 metres (49 feet)
- C. 20.5 metres (67 feet)
- D. 205 metres (673 feet)

You should be able to read the number plate on a vehicle about four or five cars away from you. And you should regard this as a minimum requirement. It is sensible to have your eyes tested regularly, especially as you get older.

Q26 **A driver can only read a number plate at the required distance with glasses on. The glasses should be worn**

Mark one answer
- A. All the time when driving
- B. Only in poor visibility
- C. Only when reversing
- D. Only when driving long distances

Q27 **You find that you need glasses to read vehicle number plates. When must you wear them?**

Mark one answer
- A. Only when you think it necessary
- B. Only in bad light or at night time
- C. Only in bad weather conditions
- D. At all times when driving

You must wear your glasses (or contact lenses) at all times when you are driving if you need them to pass the official eyesight test. If you drive without them you will be putting yourself and others at risk. Driving with uncorrected eyesight is an offence, the penalty for which could be a fine and an endorsement.

Q28 **You are about to drive home. You cannot find the glasses you need to wear when driving. You should**

Mark one answer
- A. Borrow a friend's glasses and drive home
- B. Drive home at night, so that the lights will help you
- C. Drive home slowly, keeping to quiet roads
- D. Find a way of getting home without driving

If you wear the wrong glasses you could still put people in danger and be guilty of an offence. With uncorrected eyesight, driving at night is even more difficult than driving in daylight. Try always to make good progress and drive safely.

Q29 **You are planning to drive a long distance. Which THREE things will make the journey safer?**

Mark three answers
- A. Avoid motorways
- B. Avoid travelling at night
- C. Drive slowly
- D. Ensure a supply of fresh air
- E. Make stops for refreshment

At night your view ahead may be limited by the beam of your headlights. And there is always the danger of dazzle by the headlights of oncoming vehicles. Driving slowly does not necessarily mean driving safely. In general you should try to fit in with the traffic flow according to the conditions and speed limits in force. Motorways can be very safe but you must guard against becoming bored or tired.

Q30 **Which TWO things would help keep you alert during a long journey?**

Mark two answers
- A. Finish your journey as fast as you can
- B. Keep off the motorways and use country roads
- C. Make regular stops for refreshments
- D. Make sure you get plenty of fresh air

Driving for too long and without fresh air is dangerous. Falling asleep at the wheel causes injury and death on all kinds of roads. Be safe. Break your long journey into stages and avoid heavy meals.

Q31 **Which THREE are likely to make you lose concentration while driving?**

Mark three answers
- A. Looking at road maps
- B. Looking in your wing mirror
- C. Listening to loud music
- D. Using a mobile phone
- E. Using your windscreen washers

Keep your hands on the steering wheel, your eyes on the road and your ears open when driving. A moment's loss of concentration can be the difference between life and death for you and other road users. Keep your windscreen clean. Keep your mirrors properly adjusted and use them to check on the actions of following traffic.

Q32 **Another driver does something that upsets you. You should**

Mark one answer
- A. Flash your headlights several times
- B. Let them know how you feel
- C. Sound your horn
- D. Try not to react

Q33 **A driver pulls out of a side road in front of you. You have to brake hard. You should**

Mark one answer
- A. Ignore the error and stay calm
- B. Flash your lights to show your annoyance
- C. Sound your horn to show your annoyance
- D. Overtake as soon as possible

Good drivers stay calm. They do not react angrily to the actions of bad drivers. To be a good driver you must be in control of your thoughts and actions. Remember that you cannot control what other people do. All you can do is set bad drivers a good example.

Q34 **How often should you stop on a long journey?**

Mark one answer
- A. At least every two hours
- B. At least every four hours
- C. When you need to eat
- D. When you need petrol

For some people, including new and inexperienced drivers, even a one-hour journey can be too long without a break. Instructors usually divide a lesson into sections so that pupils are not driving for one hour without a break.

Q35 **If you start to feel tired on your journey you should**

Mark one answer

- **A.** Complete the journey then have a good sleep
- **B.** Stop immediately and take deep breaths
- **C.** Stop and have a short nap or some strong coffee
- **D.** Stop and eat a large meal

A heavy meal will make you sleepy. Strong coffee could help to keep you awake but fresh air and a short rest may be all you need. Avoid too much liquid refreshment and always avoid alcoholic drinks.

Q36 **If you are feeling tired it is best to stop as soon as you can. Until then you should**

Mark one answer

- **A.** Ensure a supply of fresh air
- **B.** Gently tap the steering wheel
- **C.** Increase your speed to find a stopping place quickly
- **D.** Keep changing speed to improve concentration

There is no substitute for fresh air. Do not let the inside of your vehicle become hot and stuffy. The lack of oxygen will make you drowsy and fall asleep without warning.

Q37 **You are driving on a motorway. You feel tired. You should**

Mark one answer

- **A.** Carry on but drive slowly
- **B.** Complete your journey as quickly as possible
- **C.** Leave the motorway at the next exit
- **D.** Stop on the hard shoulder

You may stop on the hard shoulder *only if there is an emergency*. This means some danger arises *after* you join the motorway. Feeling tired is *not* an emergency in the eyes of the law because you could leave the motorway when you begin to feel drowsy.

Q38 **You should NOT drive if**

Mark one answer

○ **A.** You suffer from cramp
○ **B.** You feel tired or unwell
○ **C.** You suffer from hay fever
○ **D.** You have just passed your test

Never drive if you are tired or actually suffering from anything that affects your performance. People prone to hay fever may drive if they are not suffering from an attack or if their medication does not affect their driving. You may drive on your own as soon as you have passed your test and before you have received your full licence. However, you would be wise to take further lessons from a professional instructor before driving alone on the motorway.

Q39 **You are about to drive but you feel ill. You should**

Mark one answer

○ **A.** Take suitable medicine before driving
○ **B.** Shorten the journey if you can
○ **C.** Promise yourself an early night
○ **D.** Not drive

Never put yourself and others at risk. Medicine takes time to act. Accidents happen even on short journeys.

Q40 **Your doctor has given you a course of medicine. Why should you ask if it is OK to drive?**

Mark one answer

○ **A.** You will have to let your insurance company know about the medicine
○ **B.** Some types of medicine can cause your reactions to slow down
○ **C.** Drugs make you a better driver by quickening your reactions
○ **D.** The medicine you take may affect your eyesight

You must inform your insurance company and the DVLA of any medical condition likely to prevent you from holding a driving licence. If you have any doubt about your fitness you should consult your doctor. Remember that some medicines, including aspirin and paracetamol, may adversely affect your driving performance.

Q41 You are not sure if your cough medicine will affect your driving. What TWO things could you do?

Mark two answers
- A. Ask your doctor
- B. Ask a friend or relative for advice
- C. Check the medicine label
- D. Drive if you feel alright

Q42 You are taking drugs which are likely to affect your driving. What should you do?

Mark one answer
- A. Drive only for short distances
- B. Limit your driving to essential journeys
- C. Only drive if accompanied by a full licence holder
- D. Seek medical advice before driving

Q43 You take some cough medicine given to you by a friend. What must you do before driving?

Mark one answer
- A. Ask your friend if taking the medicine affected their driving
- B. Check the label to see if the medicine will affect your driving
- C. Drink some strong coffee
- D. Make a short journey to see if the medicine is affecting your driving

If you take medicine that might affect your driving, consult your doctor before you drive. The next best thing to do is check the label for any advice or warnings. If in doubt, do not drive.

Q44 How does alcohol affect your driving?

Mark one answer
- A. It improves your co-ordination
- B. It increases your awareness
- C. It reduces your concentration
- D. It speeds up your reactions

Q45 **What are THREE ways that drinking alcohol can affect driving?**

Mark three answers
- ○ **A.** It affects your judgement of speed
- ○ **B.** It reduces your confidence
- ○ **C.** It reduces your co-ordination
- ○ **D.** It slows down your reactions

Q46 **Which THREE result from drinking alcohol and driving?**

Mark three answers
- ○ **A.** False sense of confidence
- ○ **B.** Faster reactions
- ○ **C.** Greater awareness of danger
- ○ **D.** Less control
- ○ **E.** Poor judgement of speed

Q47 **Which THREE of these are likely effects of drinking alcohol on driving?**

Mark three answers
- ○ **A.** Colour blindness
- ○ **B.** Faster reactions
- ○ **C.** Increased concentration
- ○ **D.** Increased confidence
- ○ **E.** Poor judgement
- ○ **F.** Reduced coordination

EFFECTS OF ALCOHOL ON DRIVERS
Alcohol is a depressant. It will reduce your muscle control, blur your vision, lower your concentration and decrease your awareness especially after dark. Alcohol can give you a false confidence which makes you overestimate your driving ability and performance. You misjudge speeds and distances. And you think your reactions are faster than they really are. Even a small amount of alcohol can impair your driving.

Q48 Which one of the following is NOT affected by alcohol?

Mark one answer
- A. Coordination
- B. Judgement of speed
- C. Perception of colours
- D. Reaction time

Q49 A driver attends a social event. What precaution should the driver take?

Mark one answer
- A. Avoid busy roads after drinking alcohol
- B. Avoid drinking alcohol on an empty stomach
- C. Avoid drinking alcohol completely
- D. Drink plenty of coffee after drinking alcohol

ALCOHOL AND FOOD
Fatty food in the stomach slows the absorption of alcohol. The more slowly the alcohol is absorbed into the blood stream, the lower the maximum level attained. Therefore, eating fatty food can result in a lower level being reached. Never drink quickly on an empty stomach. But remember that even a small amount of alcohol in your blood will affect your driving. And the effects of alcohol could last for up to 12 hours after you stop drinking. NEVER DRINK AND DRIVE.

Q50 What advice should you give to a driver who has had a few alcoholic drinks at a party?

Mark one answer
- A. Drive home carefully and slowly
- B. Go home by public transport
- C. Have a strong cup of coffee and then drive home
- D. Wait a short while and then drive home

ALCOHOL FOR MEN AND WOMEN
One man is tall and fat, the other is short and thin. Both men drink a pint of beer. What happens to the alcohol level in their blood? It goes higher in the small man's blood. The same would be true if both drinkers had been women. For a man and woman of the same size and weight, the woman's level would get higher than the man's. Remember you can still be charged with a drink driving offence even if the alcohol in your blood, breath or urine is below the legal limit.

Q51 **When driving what is the maximum legal level for alcohol in your blood?**

Mark one answer

- **A.** 50 mg per 100 ml
- **B.** 60 mg per 100 ml
- **C.** 80 mg per 100 ml
- **D.** 90 mg per 100 ml

ALCOHOL AND THE LAW

35 micrograms of alcohol in 100 ml of breath or 107 milligrams of alcohol in 100 ml of urine is equivalent to the legal limit of alcohol in the blood. The penalty for driving, attempting to drive or being in charge of a vehicle while over the limit is an automatic disqualification with, possibly, imprisonment for as long as 6 months and a fine of up to £5000. And it would be an equally serious offence to fail to provide a specimen for a police laboratory test. NEVER DRINK AND DRIVE.

Q52 **What does this sign warn you to look for?**

Mark one answer
- ○ **A.** A park
- ○ **B.** A pedestrian crossing
- ○ **C.** A school crossing patrol
- ○ **D.** School children

The word **School** is usually on a plate underneath the sign to warn that you are approaching a school. If the word **Patrol** is on the plate underneath the sign, you know you are approaching a school crossing patrol. Often there is also a pair of amber lights that are flashing when the crossing patrol is actually there to control the traffic.

Q53 **How will a school crossing patrol signal you to stop?**

Mark one answer
- ○ **A.** By displaying a red light
- ○ **B.** By displaying a stop sign
- ○ **C.** By giving you an arm signal
- ○ **D.** By pointing to children on the opposite pavement

The person in charge of the crossing is authorised to control the traffic by holding up the official **STOP CHILDREN** sign. No other signal is approved.

Q54 **You are approaching a school crossing patrol. When this sign is held up you must**

Mark one answer
- ○ **A.** Stop and allow any children to cross
- ○ **B.** Stop and beckon the children to cross
- ○ **C.** Stop only if the children are on a pedestrian crossing
- ○ **D.** Stop only when the children are actually crossing the road

Q55 **You see someone step on to the road holding this sign. What must you do?**

Mark one answer

- **A.** Drive carefully round the person
- **B.** Pull up before the person
- **C.** Signal the person to cross
- **D.** Slow down and look out for children

Always approach with care any school and area such as a recreation park where there may be children. Remember that you *must stop* when you see the **STOP CHILDREN** sign.

Q56 **A school crossing patrol shows a stop children sign. What must you do?**

Mark one answer

- **A.** Continue if safe to do so
- **B.** Stop at all times
- **C.** Slow down and be ready to stop
- **D.** Stop ONLY if children are crossing

The **STOP CHILDREN** sign means you *must stop* even if you cannot see any children.

Q57 **Look at this picture. What is the danger you should be most aware of?**

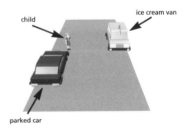

child

ice cream van

parked car

Mark one answer

- **A.** The car on the left may move off
- **B.** The child may run out into the road
- **C.** The driver of the ice cream van may get out
- **D.** The ice cream van may move off

Whenever you see an ice cream van, slow down and be prepared for children to appear from nowhere and run into the road ahead of you. Remember children are vulnerable.

Q58 **You are driving past a line of parked cars. You notice a ball bouncing out into the road ahead. What should you do?**

Mark one answer

- A. Continue driving at the same speed and flash your headlights
- B. Continue driving at the same speed and sound your horn
- C. Slow down and be prepared to stop for children
- D. Stop and wave the children across to fetch their ball

Always scan the road ahead. Look for clues to warn you of unseen hazards. Slow down especially when young children at play might run into the road. Remember they may be unaware of any danger or of your approach. Sounding your horn or flashing your lights would not help. Waving them into the road would make matters worse. See **Q112, Q424**.

Q59 **You are turning left into a side road. Pedestrians are crossing the road near the junction. You must**

Mark one answer

- A. Sound your horn
- B. Switch on your hazard lights
- C. Wait for them to cross
- D. Wave them on

You must always give priority to pedestrians in danger on the road ahead. Be patient especially if they are elderly, infirm and unaware of your pressence. See **Q112, Q424**.

Q60 **You are turning left from a main road into a side road. People are already crossing the road into which you are turning. You should**

Mark one answer

- A. Continue, as it is your right of way
- B. Signal to them to continue crossing
- C. Sound your horn to warn them of your presence
- D. Wait and allow them to cross

Try to make eye contact with other road users but never try to give them instructions. Be patient. Do not rev your engine. Do **not** sound your horn unless there is danger. See **Q112, Q424**.

Q61 You are turning left at a junction. Pedestrians have started to cross the road. You should

Mark one answer
- A. Blow your horn and proceed
- B. Give way to them
- C. Go on giving them plenty of room
- D. Stop and wave at them to cross

Q62 You are at a road junction turning into a minor road. There are pedestrians crossing the minor road. You should

Mark one answer
- A. Carry on, the pedestrians should give way to you
- B. Give way to the pedestrians who are already crossing
- C. Sound your horn to let the pedestrians know you are there
- D. Stop and wave the pedestrians across

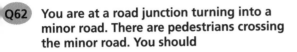

Always look out for pedestrians crossing a road you want to turn into. A pedestrian about to step into a road may wait if you signal clearly in good time and you make eye contact with the pedestrian. Remember that you are not authorised to tell other road users what to do. So never wave pedestrians to step into the road. They might obey your signal without checking and step under a bus. See **Q112, Q424**.

Q63 You are about to reverse into a side road. A pedestrian wishes to cross behind you. You should

Mark one answer
- A. Give way to the pedestrian
- B. Reverse before the pedestrian starts to cross
- C. Wave to the pedestrian to stop
- D. Wave to the pedestrian to cross

Q64 **You are reversing around a corner when you notice a pedestrian walking behind you. What should you do?**

Mark one answer
- A. Continue reversing and sound your horn
- B. Continue reversing and steer round the pedestrian
- C. Slow down and wave the pedestrian across
- D. Stop and give way

Give way to pedestrians. This rule applies whether you are driving forward or in reverse. When you are reversing, look out especially for children and elderly people. You may not see small children through your rear window. Elderly people may be slow to move out of the way.

Q65 **You see a pedestrian carrying a white stick. This shows that the person is**

Mark one answer
- A. Blind
- B. Deaf
- C. Disabled
- D. Elderly

Q66 **You see a pedestrian with a white stick and two red reflective bands. This means the person is**

Mark one answer
- A. Blind and dumb
- B. Deaf and blind
- C. Deaf and dumb
- D. Physically disabled

Take extra care with people who are blind and deaf. Usually you can tell when pedestrians are blind or blind and deaf but not when they are just deaf. Bear that in mind if a pedestrian suddenly steps into the road without looking in your direction.

Q67 You are driving in town. There is a bus at the bus stop on the other side of the road. Why should you be careful?

Mark one answer
- A. Pedestrians may come from behind the bus
- B. The bus may have broken down
- C. The bus may move off suddenly
- D. The bus may remain stationary

When in towns especially near shops, watch out for pedestrians suddenly appearing from behind parked cars and buses. Drive carefully and be prepared to slow down. See **Q20**.

Q68 Which sign means there may be people walking along the road?

Mark one answer

A

C

B

D

Q69 You are driving on a country road. What should you expect to see coming towards you on YOUR side of the road?

Mark one answer
- A. Bicycles
- B. Horse riders
- C. Motorcycles
- D. Pedestrians

The Highway Code tells pedestrians to walk on the right-hand side of the road when there is no pavement or footpath. This is so they see you and other oncoming traffic. They are advised to keep close to the side of the road. Cyclists and horse riders should also be on your side of the road but going in the same direction as yourself. Watch out at night for cyclists riding without lights.

Q70 **Your vehicle hits a pedestrian at 40 mph. The pedestrian**

Mark one answer
- A. Will certainly be killed
- B. Will probably be killed
- C. Will certainly survive
- D. Will probably survive

Driving too fast is a major cause of deaths in road traffic accidents. The speed at which a car strikes a pedestrian is crucial. The few adults surviving being hit by a car travelling at 40 mph would probably have very severe injuries. Only about 1 in 20 pedestrians would be killed if the car is travelling at 20 mph. The injuries of those not killed are likely to be slight. The risk of serious injury or death is greater for children than for adults.

Q71 **You are driving behind a cyclist. You wish to turn left just ahead. You should**

Mark one answer
- A. Go around the cyclist on the junction
- B. Hold back until the cyclist has passed the junction
- C. Overtake the cyclist before the junction
- D. Pull alongside the cyclist and stay level until after the junction

Think carefully before overtaking a cyclist especially if you are intending to turn left. Suppose you have to give way to pedestrians before you can turn. What happens when the cyclist you have just overtaken catches you up?

Q72 **You should NEVER attempt to overtake a cyclist**

Mark one answer
- A. Just before you turn left
- B. Just before you turn right
- C. On a one-way street
- D. On a dual carriageway

A cyclist is a vulnerable road user. Cutting in front of a cyclist in order to turn left is a dangerous manoeuvre that would put the cyclist at risk. What might happen if you could not complete the turn and stopped suddenly? Always give cyclists plenty of room when overtaking on a one-way street or dual carriageway and when you are going to turn right.

Q73 **When you are overtaking a cyclist, you should leave as much room as you would give to a car. Why is this?**

Mark one answer

○ **A.** The cyclist might have to make a right turn
○ **B.** The cyclist might get off the bike
○ **C.** The cyclist might change lanes
○ **D.** The cyclist might swerve

Two-wheeled vehicles, including mopeds and motorcycles, are less stable and more easily affected by the weather and road conditions than are cars and other vehicles on four wheels. Cycles form less than 3% of all vehicle traffic but are involved in 6% of all injury accidents.

Q74 **You are coming up to a roundabout. A cyclist is signalling to turn right. What should you do?**

Mark one answer

○ **A.** Give a horn warning
○ **B.** Give the cyclist plenty of room
○ **C.** Overtake on the right
○ **D.** Signal the cyclist to move across

You may see a cyclist ahead of you but other drivers may not. Your vehicle can easily hide cyclists from the view of drivers in vehicles behind you. A cyclist turning right is in more danger than a cyclist turning left.

Q75 **You are approaching the roundabout and see the cyclist signal right. Why is the cyclist keeping to the left?**

Mark one answer

○ **A.** It is a quicker route for the cyclist
○ **B.** The cyclist is going to turn left instead
○ **C.** The cyclist is slower and more vulnerable
○ **D.** The cyclist thinks the highway code does not apply to bicycles

Cyclists tend to keep out of danger by keeping well to the left-hand side of the road. If you are waiting at a junction, look out for cyclists in your blind spot and riding past on your left. Be extra careful if you intend to turn left.

Q76 **You are driving behind two cyclists. They approach a roundabout in the left-hand lane. In which direction should you expect the cyclists to go?**

Mark one answer
- **A.** Left
- **B.** Right
- **C.** Straight ahead
- **D.** Any direction

Remember that cyclists tend to keep well to the left especially on a roundabout and even when they are going to turn right. Cyclists should indicate their intentions but steering a cycle is more difficult when giving an arm signal.

Q77 **Which TWO should you allow extra room when overtaking?**

Mark two answers
- **A.** Bicycles
- **B.** Motorcycles
- **C.** Road sweeping vehicles
- **D.** Tractors

To overtake a moving vehicle you often have to move closer to vehicles coming towards you. Always think carefully before deciding to overtake. Give two-wheeled vehicles at least the same room as four-wheeled vehicles.

Q78 **You are overtaking a motorcyclist. What should you do?**

Mark one answer
- **A.** Give as much room as you would for a car
- **B.** Move over to the opposite side of the road
- **C.** Pass close by and as quickly as possible
- **D.** Try to pass on a bend

Give two-wheeled vehicles space. Never put motorcyclists at risk by driving too close. See **Q215**.

Q79 **Why should you allow extra room when overtaking a motorcyclist on a windy day?**

Mark one answer

- **A.** The rider may turn off suddenly to get out of the wind
- **B.** The rider may be blown across in front of you
- **C.** The rider may be travelling faster than normal
- **D.** The rider may stop suddenly

The weather and road conditions affect two-wheeled vehicles far more than four-wheeled vehicles. When you are alongside a motorcycle, your car may screen it from the wind. So when you and other vehicles are overtaking the motorcycle, the rider may have to cope with being blown off course by strong gusts of wind. See **Q214, Q219**.

Q80 **Where should you take particular care to look out for motorcyclists and cyclists?**

Mark one answer

- **A.** On one way streets
- **B.** On dual carriageways
- **C.** At junctions
- **D.** At zebra crossings

Two-wheeled vehicles are smaller and more difficult to see than most four-wheeled vehicles. Consequently it is easy not to notice a cyclist, moped rider or even a motorcyclist hidden in one of your blind spots. Always check for them especially if you intend to turn left.

Q81 **Where in particular should you look out for motorcyclists?**

Mark one answer

- **A.** At a road junction
- **B.** In a filling station
- **C.** Near a service area
- **D.** When entering a car park

Always look out for mopeds and motorcycles wherever you are. These two-wheeled vehicles can appear suddenly from nowhere, and you may find they are in the wrong place just as you are turning into or out of a major road.

Q82 **You are waiting to come out of a side road. Why should you watch carefully for motorcycles?**

Mark one answer
- A. Motorcycles have right of way
- B. Motorcycles are small and hard to see
- C. Motorcycles are usually faster than cars
- D. Police patrols often use motorcycles

Cars parked along a major road can make life very difficult for traffic turning out of side roads. Always look for two-wheeled vehicles that may be approaching along the major road but being hidden from your view by other traffic or parked vehicles.

Q83 **You notice horse riders in front. What should you do FIRST?**

Mark one answer
- A. Accelerate around them
- B. Be prepared to slow down
- C. Pull out to the middle of the road
- D. Signal right

Take extra care near horse riders. Slow down. Give them plenty of room. Make eye contact with the riders if possible. Drive smoothly and quietly to reduce the risk of making the horses panic and upsetting their riders. Horse and rider are both vulnerable.

Q84 **You are driving on a narrow country road. Where would you find it most difficult to see horses and riders ahead of you?**

Mark one answer
- A. On left-hand bends
- B. On right-hand bends
- C. When travelling downhill
- D. When travelling uphill

Remember that horses and riders must obey the rules of the road by travelling in the same direction as other traffic on the same side of the road. Look for other clues like fresh dung on the road to warn you of horses or other animals ahead.

Q85 **As you are driving along you meet a group of horses and riders from a riding school. Why should you be extra cautious?**

Mark one answer
- A. Many of the riders may be learners
- B. The horses will panic more because they are in a group
- C. They will be moving in single file
- D. They will be moving slowly

Look for the road sign warning of accompanied horses or ponies. This is usually found near riding stables and bridle paths. Remember that riders under 14 years of age must, by law, wear a suitable protective riding helmet.

Q86 **How should you overtake horse riders?**

Mark one answer
- A. Drive up close and overtake as soon as possible
- B. Drive slowly and leave plenty of room
- C. Speed is not important but allow plenty of room
- D. Use your horn just once to warn them

Horses may panic and shy at sudden movements and sounds. Always give horse riders a wide berth. Make eye contact with the riders if you can. Drive by slowly, smoothly and as quietly as possible. Do *not* flash your lights or sound your horn.

Q87 **What lane will horse riders take when going round a roundabout?**

Mark one answer
- A. Between centre and right
- B. Centre
- C. Left
- D. Right

Horse riders and cyclists should try to keep as far away as possible from other traffic. Be patient and expect them to stay to your left even if they give an arm signal to turn right at a junction or a roundabout.

Q88 **A horse rider is in the left lane approaching a roundabout. The driver behind should expect the rider to**

Mark one answer
- A. Go ahead
- B. Go in any direction
- C. Turn left
- D. Turn right

The Highway Code tells horse riders to keep left when they are riding, to keep the horse to their left when they are leading it and to avoid roundabouts wherever possible.

Q89 **You see some horse riders as you approach a roundabout. They are signalling right but keeping well to the left. You should**

Mark one answer
- A. Cut in front of them
- B. Keep close to them
- C. Proceed as normal
- D. Stay well back

The Highway Code tells horse riders using a roundabout to keep left but to signal right when riding across exits to show they are not leaving. Horse riders should signal left just before they leave the roundabout. And they must watch out for vehicles crossing their path to leave or join the roundabout.

Q90 **When passing animals you should NOT**

Mark one answer
- A. Change down to a lower gear
- B. Have any lights on
- C. Rev the engine or sound the horn
- D. Use your direction indicators

This question is easy if you remember that when passing by animals you should drive slowly in a lower gear, you should use sidelights between sunset and sunrise and you should use your indicators before turning left or right. Loud noise startles animals.

Q91 **Which THREE should you do when passing sheep on a road?**

Mark three answers
- **A.** Allow plenty of room
- **B.** Be ready to stop
- **C.** Briefly sound your horn
- **D.** Drive very slowly
- **E.** Pass quickly but quietly

Sheep are nervous animals. They are easily frightened by noise and sudden movement. Sheep can easily injure themselves if they bolt. If your vehicle injures a stray sheep on the road, you must report the incident to the police within 24 hours if you cannot give your name and address to the sheep's owner.

Q92 **What is the most common factor in causing road accidents?**

Mark one answer
- **A.** Driver error
- **B.** Mechanical failure
- **C.** Road conditions
- **D.** Weather conditions

95% of all road traffic accidents involve an element of human error. 65% are caused by human factors alone. Less than 5% of accidents are caused only by road conditions or by vehicle defects. Faulty tyres and brakes contribute more than mechanical defects.

Q93 **You have just passed your driving test. How likely are you to have an accident compared with other drivers?**

Mark one answer
- **A.** About the same
- **B.** It depends on your age
- **C.** Less likely
- **D.** More likely

There is no substitute for experience. But practice makes perfect only if you practise the correct techniques and develop the attitudes of the good defensive driver.

Q94 **Which age group is most likely to be involved in a road accident?**

Mark one answer
- A. 17 to 25 year-olds
- B. 36 to 45 year-olds
- C. 46 to 55 year-olds
- D. 55 year-olds and over

About 16% of all drivers and riders are aged between 17 and 25. But of all drivers and riders involved in injury accidents, about 32% are aged between 17 and 25. Young, inexperienced drivers under the age of 25 are twice as likely to be involved in accidents compared to older, more experienced drivers.

Q95 **You are following a car driven by an elderly driver. You should**

Mark one answer
- A. Flash your lights and overtake
- B. Stay close behind and drive carefully
- C. Expect the driver to drive badly
- D. Be aware that the driver's reactions may not be as fast as yours

Close following, headlight flashing and unnecessary overtaking are signs of aggressive driving. A licence grants the holder the privilege of driving on the public roads. You could lose your licence for careless, dangerous or inconsiderate driving.

Q96 **As a new driver, how can you decrease your risk of accidents on the motorway?**

Mark one answer
- A. By driving only in the nearside lane
- B. By keeping up with the car in front
- C. By never driving over 45 mph
- D. By taking further training

New learner drivers are not allowed to drive on the motorway. Newly qualified drivers are. Experience on some dual carriageways will help to prepare you for motorway driving. But there is no substitute for motorway tuition and practice under the guidance of an approved driving instructor.

Q97 You want to turn right from a junction but your view is restricted by parked vehicles. What should you do?

Mark one answer
- A. Move out quickly but be prepared to stop
- B. Sound your horn and pull out if there is no reply
- C. Stop then move slowly forward until you have a clear view
- D. Stop get out and look along the main road to check

When parked cars obstruct your view you have no choice but to 'feel your way' forward until you can be sure it is safe to turn. Remember this and think of other road users when you are choosing a safe and convenient place to park your vehicle.

Q98 The approach to a zebra crossing is marked with zigzag lines. Which TWO must you NOT do within the marked area?

Mark two answers
- A. Cross the lines
- B. Drive at more than 10 mph
- C. Overtake
- D. Park

You may exceed 10 mph and drive over the zigzag lines if the crossing is clear of pedestrians and you are not overtaking another vehicle. But always approach crossings with care and within the area marked by the zigzag lines; never park or stop, even to pick up or set down a disabled passenger. See **Q15, Q16, Q430, Q431.**

Q99 When may you stop on a pedestrian crossing?

Mark one answer
- A. Between the hours of 11pm and 7am
- B. Not at any time
- C. To avoid an accident
- D. When there is a queue of traffic in front of you

You may stop in front or behind a crossing within the area marked by the zig-zag lines. You must stop to give precedence to pedestrians, to obey pelican crossing lights or the signals from an authorised person and to avoid an accident. But you must *not* stop on the crossing itself.

Q100 **When you park your vehicle you must NOT**

Mark one answer
- **A.** Leave it in gear
- **B.** Leave the sidelights on
- **C.** Obstruct other road users
- **D.** Park on a major road

Think of the safety of pedestrians and other road users when you park. When you choose a safe and convenient place to park, your vehicle should not endanger or inconvenience others. Never leave the engine running or the headlights on. Park in reverse gear facing downhill and in a forward gear facing uphill.

Q101 **In which THREE places would parking your vehicle cause danger or obstruction to other road users?**

Mark three answers
- **A.** At or near a bus stop
- **B.** In front of a property entrance
- **C.** In a marked parking space
- **D.** On the approach to a level crossing
- **E.** On your driveway

It is an offence to cause unnecessary obstruction. It is a separate offence to leave your vehicle in a dangerous position. Where possible use an authorised parking bay or your own driveway.

Q102 **You are driving towards a zebra crossing. Pedestrians are waiting to cross. You should**

Mark one answer
- **A.** Give way to the elderly and infirm only
- **B.** Slow down and prepare to stop
- **C.** Use your headlamps to indicate they can cross
- **D.** Wave at them to cross the road

Always approach zebra crossings with caution. Look for pedestrians waiting to cross. At zebra crossings, pedestrians have absolute priority to cross once they have placed a foot on the crossing. Give pedestrians, especially the elderly and infirm, time to cross when they are on the crossing. You should treat a zebra crossing with an island as two separate crossings. But beware that pedestrians may be treating it as one crossing. See **Q14**.

Q103 You stop for pedestrians waiting to cross at a zebra crossing. They do not start to cross. What should you do?

Mark one answer
- A. Be patient and wait
- B. Drive on
- C. Sound your horn
- D. Wave them to cross

You normally do not need to stop for pedestrians waiting at a zebra crossing. If you do stop to let them cross, make eye contact, smile and be patient. Remember that you must *not* sound your horn when stationary except in an emergency. And it is dangerous to wave pedestrians into the road in case they do so without checking that it is safe. See **Q14**.

Q104 You are approaching a pelican crossing. The amber light is flashing. You must

Mark one answer
- A. Encourage pedestrians to cross
- B. Give way to pedestrians who are crossing
- C. Not move until the green light appears
- D. Stop even if the crossing is clear until the green light appears

At pelican crossings pedestrians see the green man flashing at the same time as drivers see the amber lights flashing. This tells pedestrians they should not start to cross but they will have time to finish safely if they have already started to cross. You may drive on if the crossing is clear of pedestrians even if the amber light is flashing. Always look out for pedestrians dashing across against the flashing green man. See **Q412**.

Q105 At a pelican crossing the flashing amber light means you should

Mark one answer
- A. Give way to pedestrians waiting to cross
- B. Give way to pedestrians already on the crossing
- C. Stop, if you can do so safely
- D. Stop and wait for the green light

If the amber light is flashing and pedestrians are crossing, you must stop. It may be safe for you to continue if the pedestrians are out of danger on the other side of the road and moving away from you. Always give way and wait if there is any doubt. See **Q412**.

Q106 A flashing amber light on a vehicle means

Mark one answer
- **A.** A doctor going to an emergency
- **B.** An emergency vehicle travelling fast
- **C.** A slow moving vehicle
- **D.** A security van carrying cash

Amber lights signal danger and usually flash. They are used on highway maintenance vehicles and at road works. Flashing amber is used on motorways, at pelican crossings, on some school crossing signs and at zebra crossings. On vehicles the direction indicator signals and hazard warning lights are also flashing amber.

Q107 What type of emergency vehicle is fitted with a green flashing light?

Mark one answer
- **A.** Ambulance
- **B.** Doctor's car
- **C.** Fire engine
- **D.** Road gritter

Flashing blue lights are used by the police and on ambulances, fire engines and other emergency vehicles. Doctors responding to an emergency call use a flashing green light.

Q108 A vehicle has a flashing green light. What does this mean?

Mark one answer
- **A.** A doctor is answering an emergency call
- **B.** It is a motorway police patrol vehicle
- **C.** A vehicle is carrying hazardous chemicals
- **D.** The vehicle is slow moving

Vehicles transporting hazardous chemicals do not display flashing lights but they usually carry panels displaying special hazard symbols and information about the chemicals.

Q109 You are travelling on a fast road in good conditions. How can you be sure you are following at a safe distance?

Mark one answer

- A. The distance between you and the car in front should be your braking distance
- B. The distance between you and the car in front should be twice the length of your vehicle
- C. There should be a one-second time gap between you and the car in front
- D. There should be a two-second time gap between you and the car in front

Driving too close is a major cause of accidents. Here is a way to measure the **minimum** gap. Start saying *"Only a fool breaks the two-second rule!"* when the vehicle in front of you passes a fixed position ahead. If you finish the rhyme before you reach that fixed position, you are keeping the minimum gap **for ideal driving conditions**.

Q110 A two-second gap between yourself and the car in front is sufficient when conditions are

Mark one answer

- A. Damp
- B. Foggy
- C. Good
- D. Wet

The Highway Code golden rule is: drive at a speed that allows you to stop well within the distance you can see to be clear. If you are following another vehicle, leave enough space so that you can pull up safely if the vehicle in front suddenly slows down or stops.

Q111 You are following a vehicle on a wet road. You should leave a time gap of at least

Mark one answer

- A. 1 second
- B. 2 seconds
- C. 3 seconds
- D. 4 seconds

To be safe, you should be no closer than your overall stopping distance. This distance is not a target. You should increase it in wet weather. You could use this rhyme: *"Only a fool breaks the two-second rule. And say it again when driving in rain"*.

Q112 **What should you use your horn for?**

Mark one answer
- ○ **A.** To alert others to your presence
- ○ **B.** To allow you right of way
- ○ **C.** To greet other road users
- ○ **D.** To signal your annoyance

The horn is an **emergency** signal. It distracts other road users to make them look for danger. Never use it between 11.30 pm and 7.00 am in a built-up area. Never use it when stationary unless there is danger from a moving vehicle. Think about deaf road users. See **Q58–Q62**.

Q113 **A vehicle pulls out in front of you at a junction. What should you do?**

Mark one answer
- ○ **A.** Accelerate past it immediately
- ○ **B.** Flash your headlights and drive up close behind
- ○ **C.** Slow down and be ready to stop
- ○ **D.** Swerve past it and blow your horn

Don't respond to inconsiderate road users by being inconsiderate yourself. What appears to be inconsiderate could simply be the actions of a new and inexperienced road user. Drivers should try to remember what it felt like to be a learner driver and a novice.

Q114 **You should ONLY flash your headlights to other road users**

Mark one answer
- ○ **A.** To let them know you are there
- ○ **B.** To show you are giving way
- ○ **C.** To show you are about to reverse
- ○ **D.** To tell them you have right of way

What is the effect of seeing flashing headlights? The headlights have drawn your attention to the vehicle's presence. What else can you be sure of? Only one thing – the driver's headlights work!

Q115 You are driving at the legal speed limit. A vehicle comes up quickly behind, flashing its headlights. You should

Mark one answer
- A. Accelerate to maintain a gap behind you
- B. Allow the vehicle to overtake
- C. Maintain your speed and prevent the vehicle from overtaking
- D. Touch the brakes to show your brake lights

Good drivers prefer to have bad drivers in front so they can see them and keep away from them. The only way you should influence bad drivers is by setting them a good example that they can copy. Defensive drivers do *not* respond aggressively to aggressive drivers.

Q116 The driver behind seems to be in a hurry and is very close behind you. You should

Mark one answer
- A. Move out nearer to the middle of the road
- B. Signal left and wave the driver past
- C. Slow down and allow the driver to overtake
- D. Take no action but keep to the speed limit

Can you ever know why other drivers drive the way they do? A driver may be rushing a casualty to hospital. Always play safe and let drivers in a hurry get past as soon as they can.

Q117 You are driving at the legal speed limit. A vehicle behind wants to overtake. Should you try to prevent the driver overtaking?

Mark one answer
- A. Yes, because the other driver is acting dangerously
- B. Yes, because the other driver is breaking the law
- C. No, not at any time
- D. No, unless it is safe to do so

Set other drivers a good example of defensive driving but leave them to decide whether or not to copy you. You cannot make other drivers keep within the law. If you try you may end up breaking the law yourself and causing a serious accident.

Q118 You are driving in traffic at the speed limit for the road. The driver behind is trying to overtake. You should

Mark one answer

○ **A.** Accelerate to get away from the driver behind

○ **B.** Keep a steady course and allow the driver behind to overtake

○ **C.** Move closer to the car ahead, so the driver behind has no room to overtake

○ **D.** Wave the driver behind to overtake when it is safe

Be considerate of other road users however foolish they may seem. Good defensive drivers stay within the law and do their best to keep themselves and other road users out of danger. Drive so that you can see and be seen by others. Make your intentions clear so that other road users can decide for themselves their safest course of action.

Q119 Which TWO of the following are causes of rear-end collisions?

Mark two answers

○ **A.** Driving too close to the vehicle in front

○ **B.** Not paying enough attention to the road

○ **C.** Pedestrian crossings in busy, built-up areas

○ **D.** Stopping at every junction

○ **E.** Traffic lights changing suddenly

Always leave enough space to pull up safely if the vehicle in front suddenly slows or stops. Aim your eyes high, keep them moving and look well ahead – well beyond the vehicle immediately in front of you. You can then plan your approach to junctions, pedestrian crossings, traffic lights and other hazards.

Q120 You are driving a slow-moving vehicle. There is a queue of traffic behind. You should

Mark one answer

○ **A.** Keep as far to the left as possible

○ **B.** Pull in when it is safe to do so

○ **C.** Take no action

○ **D.** Wave the traffic past when the road is clear

Holding up traffic by driving slowly can frustrate and endanger other road users. Suppose traffic builds up behind the caravan you are towing slowly up a steep hill. You could pull over when you reach the top and give the drivers a chance to go past. Let them decide if and when it is safe to overtake you.

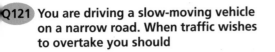

Q121 **You are driving a slow-moving vehicle on a narrow road. When traffic wishes to overtake you should**

Mark one answer

- A. Pull in safely as soon as you can
- B. Put your hazard warning lights on
- C. Stop immediately and wave them on
- D. Take no action

Q122 **You are driving a slow moving vehicle on a narrow winding road. You should**

Mark one answer

- A. Give a left signal when it is safe for vehicles to overtake you quickly
- B. Keep well out to stop vehicles overtaking dangerously
- C. Pull in safely when you can to let following vehicles overtake
- D. Wave following vehicles past you if you think they can overtake quickly

Try never to hold up traffic by driving unnecessarily slowly. If your vehicle is a slow moving tractor or agricultural vehicle, be considerate and let faster moving traffic pass where possible. But leave the decision to overtake to the drivers. Do not wave them on even though the road ahead may seem safe to you. Never signal except to indicate that you are going to stop or turn.

Q123 **You are in a one-way street and want to turn right. You should position yourself**

Mark one answer

- A. In either lane, depending on the traffic
- B. In the right-hand lane
- C. In the left-hand lane
- D. Just left of the centre line

One-way streets are to help keep traffic flowing freely. You may overtake on the left or the right but you must watch for pedestrians looking the wrong way while crossing a one-way street. Unless road markings or traffic signs indicate otherwise, the left-hand lane is for going left, the right-hand lane is for going right and the most appropriate lane according to the circumstances for going straight ahead. Choose the correct lane for your exit as soon as you can. Never change lanes suddenly.

Q124 **A bus is stopped at a bus stop ahead of you. Its right hand indicator is flashing. You should**

Mark one answer

○ **A.** Flash your headlights and slow down

○ **B.** Sound your horn and keep going

○ **C.** Slow down and give way if it is safe to do so

○ **D.** Slow down and then sound your horn

Bus drivers must try to keep to their timetable. You can help them. Remember that their large vehicles are often difficult to manoeuvre and their vision to their rear may be poor. Always drive to see and be seen. Use your horn and flash your lights only in an emergency. See **Q20**.

Q125 **You must take extra care when driving near trams because**

Mark one answer

○ **A.** Of their speed and silent approach

○ **B.** They may stop suddenly to re-charge the batteries

○ **C.** They are automatic and have no driver

○ **D.** You must NOT drive over the rails

You **must not** enter a lane or road reserved for trams. Remember that trams can be up to 60 metres (196 ft) long. Always give way to trams. Never drive between a tram and the left-hand kerb at stops without platforms. Take extra care where the track crosses from one side of the road to the other, where the road narrows and where the tracks come close to kerb. Do not park where your vehicle would obstruct trams or cause other vehicles to get in their way.

The three topics in this section are about **your vehicle**. The first is concerned with the factors affecting how your vehicle responds to your controls. The second topic explains the regulations about loading your vehicle. The third is about detecting faults which could affect your vehicle's performance and make it unsafe and also covers safety equipment.

VEHICLE HANDLING

Good drivers match how they drive to suit their vehicle and the conditions. You must know and understand what effect road and weather conditions can have upon safe speeds, braking and following distances. Saying the rhyme *"only a fool breaks the two-second rule"* will **not** give you the minimum following distance on wet or icy roads. You must also know and understand what effect the time of day and the lighting conditions could have on your driving.

Always drive so that you could if necessary stop safely within the distance you can see to be clear

VEHICLE LOADING

You need to know that it is an offence to carry in your vehicle more adult passengers than there are seats. And it can be an offence to let children sit on adult laps. If something on your roof rack overhangs your vehicle by more than two metres, you must make it obvious to other road users by attaching a projection triangle or a red cloth to the overhanging end of the load. You should also know that a heavily loaded roof rack would make your vehicle less stable and less safe. It is an offence to load your vehicle so that the load exceeds the maximum gross weight or axle weight of your vehicle.

Do not load your vehicle, carry passengers, load your roof rack or tow a trailer in such a way as to risk injury to yourself, your passengers or others

SAFETY AND YOUR VEHICLE

Good drivers develop 'car sympathy'. They drive defensively with care and consideration for their own vehicle as well as for other road users. You should become used to the way your vehicle handles and sounds. This will help you to recognise the warning signs of a fault often early enough to prevent serious damage or mechanical breakdown occurring.

Understand the instrument panel warning lights and know what action to take when any of them come on

By law, the condition of your vehicle must not constitute a danger of injury to yourself or others. It is an *absolute offence* to use a vehicle breaching the Construction and Use Regulations (CUR) even if you are unaware of the vehicle's fault. There are detailed regulations that require you to keep your vehicle's various different parts in good condition and working order. These regulations are listed in The Highway Code (in the section on the road user and the law). For a motor car over three years old, there are specific parts that must pass the Department of Transport test for the car to receive its MOT Certificate. These parts include *brakes, steering and suspension, tyres and wheels, exhaust, indicators, lights and reflectors, windscreens and washers, windows, seat belts and fittings, speedometer and horn.*

Seat belts can save lives and lessen injuries. If seat belts are fitted, you and your passengers must wear them. The driver is responsible for passengers under 14 years age. Children under 3 years old must wear an appropriate child restraint. Head restraints help to prevent serious neck injuries when the vehicle is struck from behind. An airbag fitted in the steering wheel inflates instantly to form a cushion between the driver and the steering wheel when the vehicle has a head-on collision. You should know where to put a red triangle to warn other traffic of a hazard. It should be before the hazard and at least 50 metres (164 ft) on ordinary roads or 150 metres (492 ft) on the motorway hard shoulder. You should know what extinguisher to use in the event of a fire.

We can damage our environment by driving badly and not keeping our vehicles in good condition.

Accelerating too quickly, high speed driving in low gears and harsh braking will create noise, waste fuel and wear out tyres unnecessarily. You should not use a vehicle or trailer which causes excessive noise. If you drive a vehicle with a faulty silencer and exhaust system, you are committing an offence as well as causing *noise* and *atmospheric pollution.* The horn is to warn others of your presence or danger. It is an offence to sound it when stationary or when driving in a built-up area between 11.30 pm and 7 am. It is also an offence to drive your car if the horn does not work.

Q126 **You should not drive with your foot on the clutch for longer than necessary because**

Mark one answer
- A. It increases the wear on the gearbox
- B. It increases petrol consumption
- C. It reduces your control of the vehicle
- D. It reduces the grip of the tyres

You press down the clutch pedal when changing gear and just before stopping. Your vehicle will usually slow down when you take your foot off the accelerator pedal. The engine can act as a brake when in gear but not when out of gear.

Q127 **Coasting the vehicle**

Mark one answer
- A. Improves the driver's control
- B. Makes steering easier
- C. Reduces the driver's control
- D. Uses more fuel

Use just the right amount of acceleration and the correct gear to negotiate bends and corners safely. Drive with the engine just pulling the vehicle around the curve. Do not use too much accelerator. Remember – the lower the gear the more control.

Q128 **Why is 'coasting' wrong?**

Mark one answer
- A. It will cause the car to skid
- B. It will make the engine stall
- C. The engine will run faster
- D. There is no engine braking

Applying the brakes is the only way to stop your vehicle when it is out of gear. Never drive with your foot resting on the clutch pedal. You could wear out your clutch. Plan ahead so you always have plenty of time to put your foot onto the clutch pedal.

Q129 What are THREE main reasons why 'coasting' downhill is wrong?

Mark three answers
- **A.** It could be difficult to get into gear
- **B.** It damages the engine
- **C.** It puts more wear and tear on the tyres
- **D.** Petrol consumption will be higher
- **E.** The vehicle will pick up speed
- **F.** You have less braking and steering control

Going down steep hills you are advised to keep in low gear so the engine can help the brakes to control your speed. Rolling downhill out of gear is too dangerous to justify the small saving in petrol consumption.

Q130 You are driving along a major road with many side-roads. What precaution should you take?

Mark one answer
- **A.** Keep well out near the centre of the road
- **B.** Slow down in case a vehicle pulls out
- **C.** Sound your horn as you reach each side-road
- **D.** Stop at each side-road and check for traffic

Aim to make the best progress that road and traffic conditions allow. In the UK you should drive on the left keeping to the left. Slow down if your safety line is threatened by oncoming traffic, parked vehicles or the possibilty of traffic emerging from junctions.

Q131 In which THREE of these situations may you overtake another vehicle on the left?

Mark three answers
- **A.** In slow moving traffic queues when traffic in the right hand lane is moving more slowly
- **B.** When a slower vehicle is travelling in the right hand lane of a dual-carriageway
- **C.** When approaching a motorway slip road where you will be turning off
- **D.** When you are in a one-way street
- **E.** When the vehicle in front is signalling to turn right

In general you should not overtake on the left. You may overtake on the left if you plan to turn left at the end of a one-way street. Make sure it is safe and watch for traffic moving across from the right-hand side of the street. Watch out for traffic hidden when you are overtaking on the left a vehicle signalling to turn right. See **Q6**.

Q132 You wish to overtake on a dual carriageway. You see in your mirror that the car behind has pulled out to overtake you. You should

Mark one answer
- A. Signal to tell the driver behind that you also want to overtake
- B. Signal and pull out to overtake
- C. Not signal until the car has passed
- D. Touch the brakes to show your brake lights

The repeating cycle of LAD-MSM-PSL is the basic routine of good driving. You *look* in your mirrors to *assess* the actions of following traffic in order to *decide* what you should do next. You use your *mirrors* before deciding to *signal* your intention to begin a *manœuvre*. Avoid any change in your speed and/or direction that would cause another road user to change their speed and/or direction.

Q133 You are driving in the left hand lane of a dual carriageway. Another vehicle overtakes and pulls in front of you leaving you without enough separation distance. You should

Mark one answer
- A. Continue as you are
- B. Drop back
- C. Move to the right lane
- D. Sound your horn

Always keep a safe gap between your vehicle and the one in front. The higher the speed the greater the gap. Use the two-second rule. The gap should never be less than your thinking distance. If it is less than your overall stopping distance you are taking a risk. When you have overtaken another vehicle, move back smoothly and quickly but do **not** reduce the gap from the vehicle behind by cutting back in too soon.

Q134 You see a vehicle coming towards you on a single-track road. You should

Mark one answer
- A. Do an emergency stop
- B. Put on your hazard flashers
- C. Reverse back to the main road
- D. Stop at a passing place

Single track roads usually have places where vehicles may pass one another. If the passing place is on your left you pull into it. If the passing place is on your right you pull up opposite it. Do not treat a passing place as a lay-by.

Q135 Which TWO are correct? The passing places on a single-track road are

Mark two answers
- A. To pull into if an oncoming vehicle wants to proceed
- B. To pull into if the car behind wants to overtake
- C. For stopping and checking your route
- D. For taking a rest from driving
- E. To turn the car around in, if you are lost

Be prepared to reverse back to a passing place if you encounter an oncoming vehicle on a single-track road, especially if the place behind is nearer than the one ahead. A small vehicle should normally give way to a larger vehicle. Downhill traffic should give way to uphill traffic.

Q136 Which THREE of the following will affect your stopping distance?

Mark three answers
- A. How fast you are going
- B. The street lighting
- C. The time of day
- D. The tyres on your vehicle
- E. The weather

At 30 mph on perfect road conditions the minimum overall stopping distance for an alert driver is 23 m (75 ft). At 60 mph the minimum overall stopping distance is 73 m (240 ft). If you double your speed you will at least treble your stopping distance. If the road becomes wet your stopping distance is at least doubled. And your stopping distance will be even greater if your tyres are in poor condition.

Q137 How can you best control your vehicle when driving in snow?

Mark one answer
- A. By driving in first gear
- B. By driving slowly in as high a gear as possible
- C. By keeping the engine revs high and slipping the clutch
- D. By staying in low gear and gripping the steering wheel tightly

If possible DO NOT DRIVE IN SNOW. Stay indoors. Heavy snow falling on ice-covered roads may be the worst weather conditions facing drivers. If you are caught in a snow storm, you should abandon your vehicle only as a last resort. Keep to main roads, follow other vehicles' tyre tracks and maintain a much greater than usual gap from the vehicle in front. Accelerate, steer and brake as delicately as possible in the highest appropriate gear and drive more slowly than usual. Remember to wash salt and grit from your vehicle, especially its underside, as soon as you can to reduce risk of corrosion.

Q138 **How should you drive around a bend on ice?**

Mark one answer
- ⬭ **A.** Braking as you enter the bend
- ⬭ **B.** In first gear
- ⬭ **C.** Slowly and smoothly
- ⬭ **D.** Using the clutch and brake together

You cause skidding by changing your vehicle's speed and/or direction more harshly than your tyre grip can handle. Sudden braking, sudden cornering or both may make your wheels lock. On a slippery road surface your vehicle may skid. Try to avoid skidding by accelerating gently, steering smoothly and braking progressively.

Q139 **To correct a rear wheel skid you should**

Mark one answer
- ⬭ **A.** Apply your handbrake
- ⬭ **B.** Turn away from it
- ⬭ **C.** Turn into it
- ⬭ **D.** Not turn at all

In any skid, you should keep a light grip on the steering wheel with both hands. Your first reaction should be immediately to release your brake pedal completely. For a rear wheel skid, steer left if the rear of the car is sliding to the left. Steer right if the rear of the car is sliding to the right. Never oversteer and cause a skid in the opposite direction. For a front wheel skid, release your accelerator pedal immediately. Wait for your front tyres to regain some grip before you try to steer. Remember that it is better to avoid a skid in the first place. Skidding on the public highway is not only dangerous but illegal.

Q140 **Why should you test your brakes after this hazard?**

Mark one answer
- ⬭ **A.** Because your brakes would be soaking wet
- ⬭ **B.** Because you will be driving on a slippery road
- ⬭ **C.** Because you would have driven down a long hill
- ⬭ **D.** Because you would have just crossed a long bridge

When you press your brake pedal you force together surfaces of the drum and/or disc brakes. Friction between the drum linings or between the pads and discs slows your wheels down. Your braking efficiency is reduced if the friction surfaces wear out or become coated in dirt, oil or water. Friction makes the brakes hot and helps to keep them dry.

Q141 You are following a vehicle at a safe distance on a wet road. Another driver overtakes you and pulls into the gap you had left. What should you do?

Mark one answer
- A. Drop back to regain a safe distance
- B. Flash your headlights as a warning
- C. Stay close to the other vehicle until it moves on
- D. Try to overtake safely as soon as you can

On a wet road keep at least a four-second gap from the vehicle in front. The closer you are the more danger you are in and the more spray your wipers have to deal with. Remember that overtaking is the most dangerous manoeuvre even in good conditions.

Q142 You are driving in misty weather. You can see more than 100m ahead. How can you make sure other drivers can see you?

Mark one answer
- A. Follow the vehicle in front closely
- B. Keep well out towards the middle of the road
- C. Turn on your headlights
- D. Turn on your rear fog lights

It is an offence (a) to drive in poor daytime visibility without illuminated headlights, (b) to switch on fog lights except when visibility is seriously reduced and (c) to dazzle other road users with headlamps or rear fog lights. See **Q7**.

Q143 You intend to park on a road at night without lights. Which of the following is right?

Mark one answer
- A. You must park facing opposite the traffic flow
- B. You must park at least half of your vehicle on the pavement
- C. Your vehicle must be visible from at least 10 metres (32 feet)
- D. The road must have a speed limit of 30 mph or less

When you drive towards a vehicle properly parked at night your headlights turn its rear reflectors into red warning lights. If the vehicle is parked partly on the pavement the reflectors could make you misjudge your road position. If the vehicle is facing you and its headlights are dirty, it presents a danger you may not see until it is too late.

Q144 You are on a narrow road at night.
A slower-moving vehicle ahead has
been signalling right for some time.
What should you do?

Mark one answer

- A. Flash your headlights before overtaking
- B. Overtake on the left
- C. Signal right and sound your horn
- D. Wait for the signal to be cancelled before overtaking

Be patient especially on narrow roads at night travelling behind a slow-moving vehicle. Take care always to cancel your signals after any manoeuvre so you do not to confuse other traffic.

Q145 Which TWO of the following are correct?
When overtaking at night you should

Mark two answers

- A. Be careful because you can see less
- B. Beware of bends in the road ahead
- C. Put headlights on full beam
- D. Sound your horn twice before moving out
- E. Wait until a bend so you can see the oncoming headlights

Overtaking at night is even more dangerous than overtaking in daylight. Keep your headlights dipped but remember that even these could dazzle oncoming road users. Sounding your horn is an offence between 11.30 pm and 7 am. See **Q7**.

Q146 You are overtaking a car at night.
You must be sure that

Mark one answer

- A. Your rear fog lights are switched on
- B. You do not dazzle other road users
- C. You flash your headlights before overtaking
- D. You have switched your lights to full beam before overtaking

It is extremely dangerous and an offence to dazzle other road users with your headlights. Be prepared to dip your headlights well before you enter a bend. This is especially important on a left-hand bend where your headlight beam is bound to shine into the faces of the oncoming drivers. See **Q7**.

Q147 **You are travelling at night. You are dazzled by headlights coming towards you. You should**

Mark one answer
- A. Pull down your sun visor
- B. Put your hand over your eyes
- C. Slow down or stop
- D. Switch on your main beam headlights

You can reduce the risk of being dazzled by oncoming headlights if you focus your eyes on the road ahead and towards the left-hand verge. Never look directly into oncoming headlights. Do not use your sun visor, tinted glasses or lenses. Keep your windows clean inside and out. Do not apply spray-on or other tinting materials to them. See **Q7**.

Q148 **You are dazzled by oncoming headlights when driving at night. What should you do?**

Mark one answer
- A. Brake hard
- B. Drive faster past the oncoming car
- C. Flash your lights
- D. Slow down or stop

When driving at night you must be able to stop within the distance of your headlight beam. This generally means you must drive more slowly after dark than in daylight. If you are dazzled by lights from another vehicle, you must at least slow down. Sometimes you need to pull over and stop. Although you can focus your attention on what you can see in the beam of your headlights, remember that some hazards up ahead may not be lit or easily seen. See **Q7**.

Q149 **You are driving on a well-lit motorway at night. You must**

Mark one answer
- A. Always use your headlights
- B. Use only your sidelights
- C. Always use rear fog lights
- D. Use headlights only in bad weather

At night your headlights will show up the cats' eyes which mark the lanes and edges of the motorway. Your headlights will also show up more clearly the countdown markers to exits and other road signs.

Q150 **You are travelling on a motorway at night with other vehicles just ahead of you. Which lights should you have on?**

Mark one answer
- **A.** Dipped headlights
- **B.** Front fog lights
- **C.** Main beam headlights
- **D.** Sidelights only

Use your headlights at night on motorways, even if they are well lit, and on roads with a speed limit greater than 50 mph. Always dip your headlights when there is a risk of dazzling other road users you may be following.

Q151 **You are driving on a motorway at night. You MUST have your headlights switched on unless**

Mark one answer
- **A.** The motorway is lit
- **B.** There are vehicles close in front of you
- **C.** Your vehicle is broken down on the hard shoulder
- **D.** You are travelling below 50 mph

If you break down on the motorway, you should pull onto the hard shoulder, stop as far left as possible and switch on your hazard warning lights. At night or in poor visibility, switch off your headlights but keep your sidelights on.

Q152 **You are driving on a motorway in fog. The left hand edge of the motorway can be identified by the cats' eyes. What colour are they?**

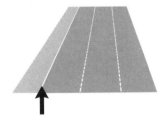

Mark one answer
- **A.** Amber
- **B.** Green
- **C.** Red
- **D.** White

See **Q347** to **Q351** and **Q433** to **Q434** inclusive.

Q153 You should only use rear fog lights when you cannot see further than about

Mark one answer

A. 100 metres (108 yds)
B. 150 metres (162 yds)
C. 200 metres (215 yds)
D. 250 metres (270 yds)

Q154 You should switch your rear fog lights on when visibility drops below

Mark one answer

A. 10 metres
B. 10 car lengths
C. 100 metres
D. Your overall stopping distance

Remember to switch off any front and rear fog lights as soon as visibility improves. They must not dazzle other road users. Always keep your windscreen and windows clean inside and out. Misty or dirty windows could make visibilty seem worse than it is.

Q155 You are following other vehicles in fog, with your lights on. How else can you reduce the chances of being involved in an accident?

Mark one answer

A. Keep close to the vehicle in front
B. Keep together with the faster vehicles
C. Reduce your speed and increase the gap
D. Use your main beam instead of dipped headlights

In fog you may not be able to see what faces the vehicle in front of yours. If you drive too close and too fast you may become part of a pile-up if the vehicles in front stop suddenly. Keep your headlights dipped. On main beam they can dazzle the driver in front and reflect back off the fog and dazzle you as well.

Q156 **You have to make a journey in foggy conditions. You should**

Mark one answer

- A. Follow closely other vehicles' tail lights
- B. Keep two seconds behind other vehicles
- C. Leave plenty of time for your journey
- D. Never use de-misters and windscreen wipers

If you must drive in fog, you must be prepared to drive more slowly than usual and to keep a greater distance from the vehicle in front than you should in perfect conditions.

Q157 **You have to make a journey in fog. What are the TWO most important things you should do before you set out?**

Mark two answers

- A. Check the battery
- B. Check your lights are working
- C. Make sure you have a warning triangle in the vehicle
- D. Make sure the windows are clean
- E. Top up the radiator with anti-freeze

Remember it is an offence to drive a vehicle with defective lights even in daytime when they are not needed. In fog you need your dipped headlights to see and be seen. You also need to clean your windscreen and windows thoroughly to help prevent them from misting up.

Q158 **You are driving in fog. The car behind seems to be very close. You should**

Mark one answer

- A. Continue cautiously
- B. Pull over and stop immediately
- C. Speed up to get away
- D. Switch on your hazard warning lights

Do not hang on the tail of the vehicle in front, especially in thick fog, unless you are travelling very slowly. If a vehicle hangs on your tail, all you can do is proceed slowly with care and try not to stop suddenly without warning.

Q159 **You are driving in fog. Why should you keep well back from the vehicle in front?**

Mark one answer
- **A.** In case its brake lights dazzle you
- **B.** In case it changes direction suddenly
- **C.** In case its fog lights dazzle you
- **D.** In case it stops suddenly

When you drive in fog you cannot clearly very far ahead. The sudden appearance of a hazard may make you to stop without being able to give much warning to traffic behind you. Even at low speeds this can lead to damaging rear-end shunts.

Q160 **Why should you always reduce your speed when driving in fog?**

Mark one answer
- **A.** Because the brakes do not work as well
- **B.** Because you could be dazzled by other people's fog lights
- **C.** Because the engine is colder
- **D.** Because it is more difficult to see events ahead

Remember the golden rule of The Highway Code: **drive at a speed that allows you to stop well within the distance you can see to be clear.**

Q161 **You have to park on the road in fog. You should**

Mark one answer
- **A.** Leave dipped headlights on
- **B.** Leave main beam headlights on
- **C.** Leave dipped headlights and fog lights on
- **D.** Leave sidelights on

It is an offence when stopped to leave headlamps on or to park without side, tail or registration plate lamps on unless unlit parking is allowed. It is extremely dangerous to park on the road in fog. If you must park in fog, you should leave on your sidelights even if you could park without lights normally.

Q162 Which THREE are suitable restraints for a child under three years?

Mark three answers
- A. An adult holding a child
- B. An adult seat belt
- C. A baby carrier
- D. A harness
- E. A lap belt

The seat belt law requires the driver and passengers of all ages in the front of the vehicle to be restrained unless exempt on medical or other grounds. Passengers travelling in the rear of cars or taxis must be restrained where a seat belt is fitted and available. Ideally, a child under three years of age should be protected by purpose-designed restraint appropriate to the child's weight. A carry cot held by straps or an infant carrier is suitable for a child under one year old. For a child over 1 but under 3 years of age an appropriate child seat or booster cushion with an adult belt is suitable. If a seat belt is not available in the rear, a child under 3 years old should be restrained by an adult.

Q163 Would it be safe to allow children to sit BEHIND the rear seats of a hatchback car?

Mark one answer
- A. Yes if you can see clearly to the rear
- B. Yes if they are under 11 years
- C. No not in any circumstances
- D. No unless all the other seats are full

Never carry children behind the rear seats of an estate car or hatchback. If you stopped suddenly in an emergency, they would be thrown forward with considerable force against the windscreen, the other passengers or yourself. This could result in severe injuries or even death.

Q164 When would it be safe for children to sit behind the rear seats in a hatchback car?

Mark one answer
- A. At any time
- B. Never
- C. On minor roads
- D. On short journeys

In the eyes of the law it is your responsibility as the driver to see that all your passengers under the age of 14 are wearing a seat belt or an appropriate child restraint.

Q165 **What do child locks in a vehicle do?**

Mark one answer

- **A.** Lock the rear windows in the up position
- **B.** Lock the seat belt buckles in place
- **C.** Stop children from opening rear doors
- **D.** Stop the rear seats from tipping forwards

Children can do what you least expect. They have been known to undo their restraint and open a door whilst the car is travelling at speed. Make sure you set the child locks of the rear doors when you have children in the back. If possible have an adult passenger with you to keep an eye on them.

Q166 **Who is responsible for making sure a vehicle is not overloaded?**

Mark one answer

- **A.** The driver of the vehicle
- **B.** The person who loaded the vehicle
- **C.** The owner of the vehicle
- **D.** The owner of the items being carried

As the driver, you are responsible for the vehicle you are driving even if you are still a new learner. You would be the one committing an offence if your vehicle is overloaded or in any way unroadworthy.

Q167 **Any load that is carried on a roof rack MUST be**

Mark one answer

- **A.** As light as possible
- **B.** Carried only when strictly necessary
- **C.** Covered with plastic sheeting
- **D.** Securely fastened when driving

Causing danger by carrying an insecure load is an offence. Luggage on a roof rack increases fuel consumption and running costs. Overloading the roof rack makes a car less stable and could provide an insurance company with a reason for not honouring a claim. If something (say a ladder) on the roof rack overhangs your vehicle by more than two metres, you must make the overhang obvious to other road users. You could fix a projection triangle or tie a red cloth to the overhanging end of the load.

Q168 **You should load a trailer so that the weight is**

Mark one answer
- A. Evenly distributed
- B. Mainly at the front
- C. Mostly at the rear
- D. Mostly over the nearside wheel

It is an offence to tow a trailer which is overloaded or which has an insecure or dangerously projecting load. When you are towing a trailer (or caravan) the national speed limit is 50 mph on single-carriageway roads and 60 mph on dual carriageways and motorways. And you must not park on the road at night without lights.

Q169 **If a trailer swerves or snakes when you are towing it, you should**

Mark one answer
- A. Brake hard and hold the pedal down
- B. Ease off the accelerator and reduce your speed
- C. Increase your speed as quickly as possible
- D. Let go of the steering wheel and let it correct itself

Q170 **How can you stop a caravan snaking from side to side?**

Mark one answer
- A. Accelerate to increase your speed
- B. Stop as quickly as you can
- C. Slow down very gradually
- D. Turn the steering wheel slowly to each side

The higher the speed the greater the risk of a caravan or trailer snaking. The maximum speed you are allowed when towing a caravan or trailer is 60 mph on dual carriageways or motorways. Remember that towing becomes more dangerous in windy conditions.

Q171 You are towing a caravan along a motorway. The caravan begins to swerve from side to side. What should you do?

Mark one answer
- A. Do an emergency stop
- B. Ease off the accelerator slowly
- C. Speed up a little
- D. Steer sharply from side to side

Experienced drivers know how to adjust their speed to the changing road conditions so that their caravan or trailer remains stable.

Q172 Your vehicle pulls to one side when braking. You should

Mark one answer
- A. Change the tyres around
- B. Consult your garage as soon as possible
- C. Pump the pedal when braking
- D. Use your handbrake at the same time

Brake pull could be caused by faulty brakes, suspension or steering. Your garage may need to readjust the brakes, tighten a component or replace friction material contaminated by grease, oil or brake fluid. If your vehicle pulls to one side when you are not braking, you should check the wear and pressure of your tyres and test for worn shock absorbers (see **Q174**).

Q173 Your vehicle pulls to one side when you brake. What is the most likely fault?

Mark one answer
- A. Incorrect tyre pressures
- B. Low brake fluid level
- C. Poorly adjusted brakes
- D. Your handbrake is still on

It is wise to check your brake fluid level weekly or when you refuel and check the engine oil level. If the fluid is leaking and you have to pump your pedal or push it an unusually long way down before your brakes work, take the car to your garage. Take notice of other symptoms of brake faults such as grab, fade, judder and squeal. It is very dangerous and an offence to drive a vehicle with defective brakes.

Q174 You are testing your suspension. You notice that your vehicle continues to bounce when you press down on the front wing. What does this mean?

Mark one answer
- A. Steering wheel not located centrally
- B. Tyres under-inflated
- C. Worn shock absorber(s)
- D. Worn tyres

Good defensive drivers become used to the way their car handles and sounds. They can usually feel and hear the warning signs of a fault developing. When you detect a fault, take steps to prevent any serious damage or mechanical breakdown. As part of the MOT test the category Steering and Suspension includes steering control, wheel alignment, shock absorbers, wheel bearings, front and rear suspension.

Q175 **It is essential that tyre pressures are checked regularly. When should this be done?**

Mark one answer
○ **A.** After any lengthy journey
○ **B.** After driving at high speed
○ **C.** When tyres are cold
○ **D.** When tyres are hot

The pressure recommended for a cold tyre allows for the increase in pressure when the tyre and the air inside it warm up on a journey. Check your tyres daily for signs of damage or excessive wear. A tyre needs repair if you have to inflate it every day.

Q176 **Why should tyres be kept to the pressure the manufacturer tells you?**

Mark one answer
○ **A.** To keep the car the right height above the road
○ **B.** To make the ride more comfortable
○ **C.** To prevent the car from skidding
○ **D.** To stop the car from leaning to one side

Tyres are your vehicle's contact with the road. If the pressure is too low, the tyre wall rapidly weakens and causes the tyre to fail. Higher tyre pressures are generally recommended for a heavily loaded car or for long journeys at high speeds. But you should avoid too high a pressure as it dangerously reduces the area of contact between the tyres and the road.

Q177 **The legal minimum depth of tread for car tyres is**

Mark one answer
○ **A.** 1 mm
○ **B.** 1.6 mm
○ **C.** 2.5 mm
○ **D.** 4 mm

This minimum tread depth must be continuous around the tyre and across the centre three-quarters of its width. For vehicles other than cars, light vans and light trailers, the minimum tread depth is 1 mm.

Q178 **Which TWO are badly affected if the tyres are under inflated?**

Mark two answers
- **A.** Braking
- **B.** Changing gear
- **C.** Reversing
- **D.** Steering

It is an offence to drive a vehicle with low tyre pressures. Your car becomes difficult to control and your overall stopping distances increase. You could lose up to 13% tread mileage if your tyre pressure is only 90% of the manufacturer's recommended value.

Q179 **Excessive or uneven tyre wear can be caused by faults in which THREE?**

Mark three answers
- **A.** The accelerator
- **B.** The braking system
- **C.** The exhaust system
- **D.** The gearbox
- **E.** The suspension
- **F.** Wheel alignment

Harsh acceleration and braking, sharp cornering at high speeds and other forms of bad driving on the public highway can cause excessive and uneven tyre wear. Good drivers inspect their tyres regularly for symptoms of possible faults with their wheels, suspension and braking systems. It always pays to keep your front wheels balanced and the tracking properly adjusted.

Q180 **It is illegal to drive with tyres that**

Mark one answer
- **A.** Are of different makes
- **B.** Have been bought second-hand
- **C.** Have a cut in the side wall
- **D.** Have painted walls

Ideally all the tyres fitted to your vehicle should be of the same make and have the same pattern with the same amount of tread. Radial tyres have walls flexible enough to allow an even road contact especially when cornering. Some radials have steel bracing. Others have textile bracing. The two types must never be mixed on the same axle. If used in combination, steel radials must be fitted to the rear wheels and the textile radials fitted to the front wheels. The earlier crossply tyre is incompatible with the more common radial tyre. Do not mix them and never on the same axle.

Q181 Which THREE does the law require you to keep in good condition?

Mark three answers
- A. Engine
- B. Gears
- C. Headlights
- D. Seat belts
- E. Windscreen

If your car is more than 3 years old, your lights, windscreen. seat belts and their anchorage will be examined as part of its MOT test. You must keep your windscreen clean and clear. It is an offence to drive with a defective lights even in daylight and with a dirty or obscured windscreen.

Q182 Which FOUR of these must be in good working order for your car to be roadworthy?

Mark four answers
- A. Horn
- B. Oil warning light
- C. Speedometer
- D. Temperature gauge
- E. Windscreen washers
- F. Windscreen wipers

You should test your horn and washers daily. It is an offence to drive with defective windscreen washers or with an empty washer bottle. Not only must your speedometer work, it must also be accurate to within 10%. Never use its possible inaccuracy as an excuse to break speed limits.

Q183 Which of these, if allowed to get low, could cause an accident?

Mark one answer
- A. Anti-freeze level
- B. Battery water level
- C. Brake fluid level
- D. Radiator coolant level

You should keep your radiator topped up with water and be sure to include anti-freeze for the winter months. If your battery is not a sealed unit you should keep it topped up with distilled water. See also **Q173**.

Q184 **When are you allowed to drive if your brake lights do NOT work?**

Mark one answer
- **A.** At no time
- **B.** During the daytime
- **C.** In an emergency
- **D.** When going for an MOT test

You signal to traffic behind you every time you press the brake pedal. So use your mirror before you do. Remember MSM (Mirror-Signal-Manoeuvre) whenever you intend to change speed and/or direction.

Q185 **If you notice a strong smell of petrol as you drive along, you should**

Mark one answer
- **A.** Carry on at a reduced speed
- **B.** Expect it to stop in a few miles
- **C.** Not worry, as it is only exhaust fumes
- **D.** Stop and investigate the problem

Bear in mind that there is always a risk of fire with petrol and its vapour. When you refuel take care never to overfill the tank. Always replace the petrol cap firmly. Remember it is an offence to drive a vehicle emitting excessive fumes.

Q186 **What should you NEVER do at a petrol station?**

Mark one answer
- **A.** Eat
- **B.** Run about
- **C.** Smoke
- **D.** Wash windscreens

The greatest danger at petrol stations is fire. Mixtures of air and petrol vapour can be explosive and set off by a naked flame or a glowing cigarette end. An electrical spark explodes petrol/air mixtures in your engine to drive your car. Remember always to switch off your engine when you and other drivers are refuelling.

Q187 **In which of these containers may you carry petrol in a motor vehicle?**

A

B

C

D

Mark one answer

○ **A.** A
○ **B.** B
○ **C.** C
○ **D.** D

Try to plan any journey so that you do not need to carry extra fuel. The greater your car load the more fuel your engine will use. The fuel in your tank is part of your car's load. If you are only making short journeys it is more economical **not** to keep your tank full up.

Q188 **It is important to wear suitable shoes when you are driving. Why is this?**

Mark one answer

○ **A.** To enable you to make quicker gear changes
○ **B.** To enable you to walk for assistance if you breakdown
○ **C.** To maintain safe control of the pedals
○ **D.** To prevent wear on the pedal rubbers

The law allows you to drive in bare feet but it is not recommended. Try to keep for driving a pair of comfortable, flat-heeled shoes with non-slip soles of medium thickness. Very thin soles can be tiring. Very thick soles can make it difficult to 'feel' the pedals.

Q189 **What is the most important factor in avoiding running into the car in front?**

Mark one answer

○ **A.** Always driving at a steady speed
○ **B.** Having tyres that meet the legal requirements
○ **C.** Keeping the correct separation distance
○ **D.** Making sure your brakes are efficient

Good drivers adjust their speed to maintain a safe distance from the vehicle in front. If your brakes develop a fault when you are out driving you will certainly need to increase the gap between you and the vehicle in front. Remember it is dangerous and against the law to drive with defective brakes and faulty tyres.

Q190 **What will cause high fuel consumption?**

Mark one answer
A. Accelerating around bends
B. Driving in high gears
C. Late harsh braking
D. Poor steering control

You could save at least 15% on your fuel bill by planning your driving. Good drivers avoid harsh acceleration and braking. For more economical and environmentally friendly motoring you should drive at appropriate, modest speeds in the highest suitable gear.

Q191 **You cannot see clearly behind when reversing. What should you do?**

Mark one answer
A. Ask someone to guide you
B. Look in the nearside mirror
C. Open the door and look behind
D. Open your window to look behind

Because part of the road you are reversing along will be hidden in your blind spots, there is always the risk of running over pedestrians – particularly children. Always reverse with great care and, wherever possible, get someone to guide you back.

Q192 **A car driver MUST ensure that seat belts are worn by**

Mark one answer
A. All front seat passengers
B. All rear seat passengers
C. All passengers
D. Children under 14

The seat belt law requires the driver and passengers of all ages in the front of the vehicle to be restrained unless exempt on medical or other grounds. Passengers travelling in the rear of cars or taxis must be restrained where a seat belt is fitted and available. Drivers are responsible for themselves and for any children under 14 years of age.

Q193 **You are carrying two children and their parents in your car. Who is responsible for seeing that the children wear seat belts?**

Mark one answer
- **A.** The children
- **B.** The children's parents
- **C.** The front seat passenger
- **D.** You

If you are driving the car, even if you are a learner under supervision, you are responsible for ensuring that any children under the age of fourteen are wearing seat belts if fitted. When there are insufficient belts for the rear seat passengers, it is safer for adults to be restrained. For children aged 1 to 4 years old, it is safer for them to wear an adult belt alone rather than no restraint at all.

Q194 **Car passengers MUST wear a seat belt if one is available, unless they are**

Mark one answer
- **A.** Exempt for medical reasons
- **B.** Sitting in the rear seat
- **C.** Under 14 years old
- **D.** Under 5 feet in height

Seat belts must be available for the driver and front seat passengers. All cars built after 1981 have anchorage points for rear seat belts. And nowadays, cars are supplied with rear seat belts fitted. Since the 1st July 1991 the law requires adults in the rear to wear seats belts if fitted.

Q195 **What will reduce the risk of neck injury resulting from a collision?**

Mark one answer
- **A.** An air-sprung seat
- **B.** Anti-lock brakes
- **C.** A collapsible steering wheel
- **D.** A properly adjusted head restraint

A whiplash injury to the neck usually happens when a stationary car is struck from behind by another vehicle. Bones in the neck can be damaged or fractured. Discs between the bones can be displaced. Nerves in the spinal column can be injured. A suitable headrest can prevent the head being jerked backwards.

Q196 **What does this warning light on the instrument panel mean?**

Mark one answer
- ○ **A.** Handbrake on
- ○ **B.** Hazard flashers
- ○ **C.** Main beam
- ○ **D.** Warning triangle

The lights on an instrument panel are usually red for danger, orange for caution and green for working. Although green is the colour of panel lights for direction indicators, side lights or dipped headlights, blue is usually the colour to show headlights are on main beam. You should find explanations of the standard symbols and panel lights in the owners manual provided with your car by the manufacturer.

Q197 **For which TWO of these may you use hazard warning lights?**

Mark two answers
- ○ **A.** When driving on a motorway, to warn drivers behind of a hazard ahead
- ○ **B.** When you are double-parked on a two-way road
- ○ **C.** When your direction indicators are not working
- ○ **D.** When your vehicle has broken down and is causing an obstruction
- ○ **E.** When warning oncoming traffic that you intend to stop

Q198 **When may you use hazard warning lights?**

Mark one answer
- ○ **A.** To park alongside another car
- ○ **B.** To park on double yellow lines
- ○ **C.** When you have broken down
- ○ **D.** When you are being towed

Hazard warning lights are for use in an emergency. They are your four indicator lights all flashing in unison. The flashing amber lights warn other road users of your presence and of a likely obstruction to their progress. Using hazard warning lights does not allow you to park illegally or ignore parking restrictions.

Q199 **Hazard warning lights should be used when vehicles are**

Mark one answer
- **A.** Being towed along a road
- **B.** Broken down and causing an obstruction
- **C.** Faulty and moving slowly
- **D.** Reversing into a side road

You use hazard warning lights in an emergency. Normally you are not moving, and are causing a temporary obstruction because your vehicle has broken down. You may use them when moving only if you are on a motorway or unrestricted dual carriageway and you need to warn drivers behind you of a hazard or obstruction up ahead. See **Q265** to **Q268**.

Q200 **When must you use dipped headlights during the day?**

Mark one answer
- **A.** All the time
- **B.** Along narrow streets
- **C.** In poor visibility
- **D.** When parking

Use dipped headlights in poor daytime visibility so that other road users can see you. Remember it is an offence not to use them and an offence to dazzle other road users with undipped headlights.

Q201 **You must NOT sound your horn**

Mark one answer
- **A.** At any time in a built-up area
- **B.** Between 10 pm and 6 am in a built-up area
- **C.** Between 11.30 pm and 6 am on any road
- **D.** Between 11.30 pm and 7 am in a built-up area

It is normally an offence to sound your horn if you car is not moving or if you are in a built-up area between 11.30 pm and 7 am.

Q202 **When should you NOT use your horn in a built up area?**

Mark one answer

○ **A.** Between 9.00 pm and dawn
○ **B.** Between dusk and 8.00 am
○ **C.** Between 8.00 pm and 8.00 am
○ **D.** Between 11.30 pm and 7.00 am

You may sound your horn or flash your lights to warn others of your presence when there is danger from another moving vehicle. After dark it may be more appropriate just to flash your lights. Never sound your horn as a greeting or to express your annoyance. See also **Q21** and **Q424**.

The three topics in this section are about **other vehicles**, **accident risks** and **safety**. The first concerns other vehicle characteristics. The second topic relates safety to weather and road conditions. The last two are about accident risks and accident handling.

OTHER TYPES OF VEHICLE

Motorcycles, articulated lorries, buses, coaches and high-sided vans all differ in their manoeuvrability and in the size of the driver's field of vision. They need different times and distances to speed up, slow down and stop. Road and weather conditions can have different effects on different vehicles. Some vehicles can worsen the effects of road and weather conditions on other vehicles. A large lorry may throw spray on to following vehicles and suddenly alter the wind force on passing vehicles. Good drivers bear these factors in mind when assessing the risks of approaching hazards.

SAFETY MARGINS

Good drivers know the correct stopping distances and how changing conditions can affect safety margins. You need to know how to cope with snow, ice or fog. You also need to know what to do if you encounter flooding or a ford. We should drive more slowly after dark than we do in daylight so that we could stop safely within the distance visible in our headlights.

ACCIDENTS

Some road users are more at risk than others. Pedestrians are very vulnerable especially if they are children, elderly, disabled or impaired. You should know that a pedestrian carrying a white stick with two red reflective bands is blind and deaf. You should allow for the possibility that a pedestrian may not see you, may misjudge your speed or may be unable to react quickly enough to your approach. If hit by a car travelling at 20 mph, a pedestrian will be injured, not always seriously, or may be killed. If hit at 40 mph, the pedestrian is usually killed. Any surviving pedestrian will usually have very serious injuries. Cyclists or horse riders, especially if they are children, are at risk on the road. You must know what to do if you meet them.

At a traffic accident there is always a risk of danger to yourself and others from *fire* and *further collisions*. Use your hazard warning lights and red triangle to warn other traffic. Make sure someone calls the emergency services, no one smokes and everyone switches off their engine. Do not move any casualties unless they are in danger. If a casualty has widely dilated pupils their heart may have stopped beating. Give priority to resuscitating anyone who has stopped breathing and to helping anyone who is bleeding heavily. Do **not** give casualties anything to drink.

By law you **must stop** if you are involved in an accident which causes damage or injury. You must give your name, address and vehicle registration number to anyone with reasonable grounds for requiring them. If you even slightly damage a parked vehicle and there is no one present at the scene, you must report the accident *in person* to the police as soon as possible and certainly within no more than 24 hours. If someone is injured, you must show your insurance certificate to the police at the time of the accident or take it to a police station within 24 hours. You should report the details of any accident to your insurance company even if you will not be making a claim against your insurance. Always follow the procedures recommended by your insurers when you record details of the accident and take names, addresses and statements from any witnesses.

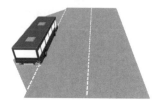

Q203 When you approach a bus signalling to move off from a bus stop you should

Mark one answer
- ◯ **A.** Allow it to pull away if safe
- ◯ **B.** Flash your headlights as you approach
- ◯ **C.** Get past before it moves
- ◯ **D.** Signal left and wave the bus on

Buses run to a timetable. The Highway Code tells you to give way to them "whenever you can do so safely, especially when they signal to pull away from bus stops". Remember to look out for passengers leaving the bus and stepping into the road.

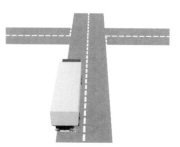

Q204 You are following a long vehicle approaching a crossroads. The driver signals right but moves close to the left-hand kerb. What should you do?

Mark one answer
- ◯ **A.** Overtake on the right-hand side
- ◯ **B.** Report the driver to the police
- ◯ **C.** Wait behind the long vehicle
- ◯ **D.** Warn the driver of the wrong signal

When turning left or right at junctions and when dealing with roundabouts, buses, coaches and articulated lorries are forced to take a different path to that of the car. These long vehicles may signal right but swing out to the left before turning. This may seem strange to a new driver.

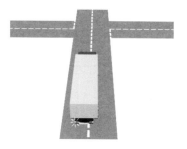

Q205 You are following a long vehicle. It approaches a crossroads and signals left but moves out to the right. You should

Mark one answer
- ◯ **A.** Assume the signal is wrong and it is really turning right
- ◯ **B.** Get closer in order to pass it quickly
- ◯ **C.** Overtake as it starts to slow down
- ◯ **D.** Stay well back and give it room

Q206 **You are approaching a mini-roundabout. The long vehicle in front is signalling left but positioned over to the right. You should**

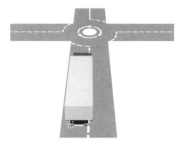

Mark one answer
- ◯ **A.** Follow the same course as the lorry
- ◯ **B.** Keep well back
- ◯ **C.** Overtake on the left
- ◯ **D.** Sound your horn

A large vehicle is forced to follow a different course to that of the car when turning at junctions and dealing with roundabouts. An articulated lorry may be signalling to go in one direction while swinging out towards the opposite direction.

Q207 **You are following a large articulated vehicle. It is going to turn left into a narrow road. What action should you take?**

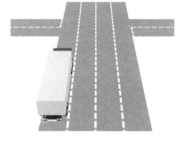

Mark one answer
- ◯ **A.** Be prepared to stop behind
- ◯ **B.** Move out and overtake on the offside
- ◯ **C.** Overtake quickly before the lorry moves out
- ◯ **D.** Pass on the left as the vehicle moves

A large vehicle not only takes up far more of the road than a car does, it also takes more time to speed up and more time to slow down. You should appreciate the problems facing the drivers of large vehicles and make allowances when you encounter such vehicles.

Q208 **Why is passing a lorry more risky than passing a car?**

Mark one answer
- ◯ **A.** The brakes of lorries are not as good
- ◯ **B.** Lorries are longer than cars
- ◯ **C.** Lorries may suddenly pull up
- ◯ **D.** Lorries climb hills more slowly

When you overtake a long lorry your car is likely to be further across on the wrong side of the road and for a longer time than it would be when you overtake another car. Two cars coming towards each other at 60 mph will be closing the gap between them at 120 mph and getting 176 ft closer together every second. If you need only four extra seconds to overtake a lorry, you would need to be at least an extra 50 car lengths away from the oncoming car.

Q209 Before overtaking a large vehicle you should keep well back. Why is this?

Mark one answer
- ◯ **A.** To give acceleration space to overtake quickly on blind bends
- ◯ **B.** To get the best view of the road ahead
- ◯ **C.** To leave a gap in case the vehicle stops and rolls back
- ◯ **D.** To offer other drivers a safe gap if they want to overtake you

It is difficult to see what traffic is in front of a large vehicle, especially if you are close behind. Good drivers stay well back to give themselves a clearer view of oncoming traffic. Bad drivers stay close up and then risk moving into the centre of the road to see oncoming traffic.

Q210 The FIRST thing you should do when you want to overtake a large lorry is

Mark one answer
- ◯ **A.** Flash your headlights and wait for the driver to wave you on
- ◯ **B.** Keep in close to the left hand side
- ◯ **C.** Move close behind so you can pass quickly
- ◯ **D.** Stay well back to get a better view

The normal driving routine of **M**irror-**S**ignal-**M**anoeuvre-**P**osition-**S**peed-**L**ook does **not** apply to overtaking. If you really must overtake another moving vehicle you need to get into the best position and speed to look for oncoming traffic: **P-S-L**. At the appropriate moment you use your mirror to check again on the traffic behind you before you signal your intention to move out and overtake: **M-S-M**.

Q211 You wish to overtake a long slow-moving vehicle on a busy road. You should

Mark one answer
- ◯ **A.** Flash your headlights for the oncoming traffic to give way
- ◯ **B.** Follow it closely and keep moving out to see the road ahead
- ◯ **C.** Keep well back until you can see it is clear
- ◯ **D.** Wait behind until the driver waves you past

You should not act on the signals of other drivers unauthorised to give them. Remember it is your responsibility to ensure that it is safe to proceed. This applies even when you have been given the signal by a police officer or some other authorised person.

Q212 When about to overtake a long vehicle you should

Mark one answer

○ **A.** Drive close to the lorry in order to pass more quickly

○ **B.** Flash your lights and wait for the driver to signal when it is safe

○ **C.** Sound the horn to warn the driver you are there

○ **D.** Stay well back from the lorry to obtain a better view

When you keep well back from any large vehicle, you only need to move very slightly to your right to get an even better view of oncoming traffic on the opposite side of road. Use your mirror before changing position. Signal when you intend to overtake.

Q213 You are following a large lorry on a wet road. Spray makes it difficult to see. You should

Mark one answer

○ **A.** Drop back until you can see better

○ **B.** Keep close to the lorry, away from the spray

○ **C.** Put your headlights on full beam

○ **D.** Speed up and overtake quickly

Remember that your overall stopping distances on wet roads are at least double what they are on dry roads. Heavy spray from vehicles often acts like fog. It stops you from seeing oncoming traffic ahead on the other side of the road.

Q214 You are driving on a wet motorway with surface spray. You should

Mark one answer

○ **A.** Drive in any lane with no traffic

○ **B.** Use dipped headlights

○ **C.** Use your hazard flashers

○ **D.** Use your rear fog lights

When motorways are wet, the spray from traffic can produce foggy conditions. When this happens you should make sure that your vehicle can be seen by others. Do not use fog lights unless visibility is below 100 metres. Do not use hazard lights except in an emergency to warn others of danger up ahead. See **Q79**.

Q215 Motorcyclists are more vulnerable than car drivers because they

Mark one answer
- **A.** Are affected more by changes in road surface
- **B.** Can accelerate faster than cars
- **C.** Ride at higher speeds
- **D.** Take corners at higher speeds

One or both wheels of a cycle or motorcycle tilt at an angle to the ground when the rider changes direction. Consequently, two-wheeled vehicles are more at risk of sliding and skidding than are vehicles on four wheels. This risk increases in wet conditions and on certain types of road surface. See **Q78**.

Q216 The road is wet. Why might a motorcyclist steer round drain covers on a bend?

Mark one answer
- **A.** To avoid puncturing the tyres on the edge of the drain covers
- **B.** To avoid splashing pedestrians on the pavement
- **C.** To help judge the bend using the drain covers as marker points
- **D.** To prevent the motorcycle sliding on the metal drain covers

Road-holding depends upon friction between the tyres and the road surface. Water, oil and other liquids can drastically reduce tyre grip on smooth surface where friction is already low.

Q217 Which of these vehicles is LEAST likely to be affected by crosswinds?

Mark one answer
- **A.** Cars
- **B.** Cyclists
- **C.** High-sided vehicles
- **D.** Motorcyclists

Two-wheeled vehicles are easily blown off course by strong crosswinds. Remember this and give cyclists and motorcyclists extra room when overtaking them. High-sided vehicles can become unstable in strong winds. Caravans and tall vans are sometimes blown over on to their side.

Q218 In which THREE places could a strong crosswind affect your course?

Mark three answers

○ **A.** After overtaking a large vehicle
○ **B.** In towns
○ **C.** In tunnels
○ **D.** On exposed sections of roadway
○ **E.** When passing gaps in hedges
○ **F.** When passing parked vehicles

A strong wind is more dangerous when it blows in gusts especially on exposed open roads. On a windy day you may experience the effect of gusting when you pass by large vehicles or gaps in hedges. In these conditions you need good control of your steering.

Q219 It is very windy. You are behind a motorcyclist who is overtaking a high-sided vehicle. What should you do?

Mark one answer

○ **A.** Keep well back
○ **B.** Keep close to the motorcyclist
○ **C.** Overtake the motorcyclist immediately
○ **D.** Stay level with the motorcyclist

Motorcyclists may easily be blown off course by a strong gust as they overtake large vehicles shielding them from crosswinds. Even your car could briefly shield a two-wheeled vehicle from a crosswind. Always give motorcycles at least the same room that you would give another car. See **Q79**.

Q220 **You are at a junction with limited visibility. You should**

Mark one answer
- A. Be ready to move off quickly
- B. Inch forward, looking to the left
- C. Inch forward, looking to the right
- D. Inch forward, looking both ways

The majority of road accidents occur at junctions. The major cause is drivers looking but not really seeing and properly assessing the dangers. At junctions you should give priority to pedestrians on the road and to traffic on the major road. The usual order of priority is

PRIORITY	GIVEN TO TRAFFIC TURNING
FIRST	left *into* a junction
SECOND	left *out of* a junction
THIRD	right *into* a junction
FOURTH	right *out of* a junction

Q221 **You are driving in a built-up area. You approach a speed hump. You should**

Mark one answer
- A. Move across to the left hand side of the road
- B. Slow your vehicle right down
- C. Stop and check both pavements
- D. Wait for any pedestrians to cross

Speed kills. Traffic calming systems and speed limits of 20 mph or less are being introduced to reduce the risk of accidents to pedestrians. Always take extra care in the vicinity of young children, the elderly and the infirm. Drive very slowly over any speed hump, keeping your foot completely away from the accelerator pedal just as you do so.

Q222 **When approaching a right-hand bend you should keep well to the left. Why is this?**

Mark one answer
- ○ **A.** It improves your view of the road
- ○ **B.** It lets faster traffic from behind overtake
- ○ **C.** To be positioned safely if the vehicle skids
- ○ **D.** To overcome the effect of the road's slope

Right-hand bend to you is a left-hand bend for traffic coming the other way. If you keep well to your left, you will improve your view of the road ahead and be at less risk from oncoming traffic taking their left-hand bend too wide.

Q223 **You are coming up to a right-hand bend. You should**

Mark one answer
- ○ **A.** Keep well to the right to avoid anything in the gutter
- ○ **B.** Keep well to the right to make the bend less sharp
- ○ **C.** Keep well to the left for a better view around the bend
- ○ **D.** Keep well to the left as it makes the bend faster

Keep well away from any hazard lines along the centre of the road especially on a bend. Never cross them to 'smooth out a corner'. They are there to separate the traffic. It is extremely dangerous and usually an offence to cross double white lines, especially if both are unbroken.

Q224 **You wish to park facing downhill. What THREE things should you do?**

Mark three answers
- ○ **A.** Park close to the bumper of another car
- ○ **B.** Put the handbrake on
- ○ **C.** Put the vehicle into reverse gear
- ○ **D.** Park with two wheels up on the kerb
- ○ **E.** Turn the steering wheel towards the kerb

It is an offence to park on a pavement even with just two wheels on the kerb. Your vehicle would be an obstruction to pedestrians and a serious hazard to someone who is blind. Park in reverse gear facing downhill. If there is a kerb, turn your steering wheel towards it. If there is a soft verge or no kerb, turn your steering wheel towards the verge. Should your parking brakes fail, your car should be set to roll off the road. It must not roll on to and across the road towards oncoming traffic.

Q225 **You are about to go down a steep hill. To control the speed of your vehicle you should**

Mark one answer

- A. Select a high gear and use the brakes carefully
- B. Select a high gear and use the brakes firmly
- C. Select a low gear and use the brakes carefully
- D. Select a low gear and avoid using the brakes

Engine braking means keeping in gear and off the accelerator pedal. It does **not** mean selecting a lower gear and letting up the clutch pedal while the road speed of the vehicle is too high for the new gear. Always change to your new gear when your road speed is appropriate for it. Poor gear changing wears out a clutch which is expensive to replace.

Q226 **You are on a long downhill slope. What should you do to help control the speed of your vehicle?**

Mark one answer

- A. Grip the steering wheel tightly
- B. Put the clutch down
- C. Select a low gear
- D. Select neutral

Never coast downhill. Keep in gear so that you have engine braking as well as your foot brakes. The lower the gear the stronger the engine braking. Remember that unnecessary coasting is dangerous and an offence.

Q227 **In very hot weather, the road surface can get soft. Which TWO of the following will be affected most?**

Mark two answers

- A. The brakes
- B. The steering
- C. The suspension
- D. The windscreen

Your control over your car's speed and direction depends upon the grip of your tyres on the road. Any change of road surface affecting tyre grip will affect your steering and braking. A firm surface gives more grip than a soft surface. A dry surface gives more grip than a wet one.

Q228 **In windy conditions you need to take extra care when**

Mark one answer
- ⬭ **A.** Making a hill start
- ⬭ **B.** Passing pedal cyclists
- ⬭ **C.** Turning into a narrow road
- ⬭ **D.** Using the brakes

Two-wheeled vehicles are more easily blown off course than other vehicles. Young children on bicycles are more vulnerable than adults on cycles or riders on mopeds and motorcycles.

Q229 **Where are you most likely to be affected by a crosswind?**

Mark one answer
- ⬭ **A.** On a busy stretch of road
- ⬭ **B.** On a long, straight road
- ⬭ **C.** On an open stretch of road
- ⬭ **D.** On a narrow country lane

Traffic on a busy road and hedges along country lanes can give you some protection from cross-winds. On long, straight roads you can adjust your steering to allow for a crosswind. Driving along an open stretch of road on a windy day needs care especially as the wind will change direction when the road changes direction.

Q230 **You are on a fast open road in good conditions. For safety the distance between you and the vehicle in front should be**

Mark one answer
- ⬭ **A.** One car length
- ⬭ **B.** Two metres (seven feet)
- ⬭ **C.** Two car lengths
- ⬭ **D.** A two-second time gap

See **Q109**, **Q110** and **Q111**. The rhyme *"Only a fool breaks the two-second rule!"* works for alert drivers in good conditions. It would not leave them enough space to pull up safely if the vehicle ahead stopped suddenly in bad conditions. Stopping distances are at least double on wet roads and up to ten times longer on icy roads.

Q231 **Stopping in good conditions at 30mph takes at least**

Mark one answer
- ⬭ **A.** 6 car lengths
- ⬭ **B.** 2 car lengths
- ⬭ **C.** 3 car lengths
- ⬭ **D.** 1 car length

Your overall stopping distance = your thinking distance + braking distance.

SPEED (MPH)	THINKING DISTANCE (M)	BRAKING DISTANCE (M)	SHORTEST STOPPING DISTANCE (M)
20	6	6	12
30	9	14	23
40	12	24	36
50	15	38	53
60	18	55	73
70	21	75	96

Learn to judge your stopping distances when you are out in traffic.

Q232 You are on a good dry road surface and in a vehicle with good brakes and tyres. What is the shortest overall stopping distance at 40 mph?

Mark one answer
- A. 23 metres (75 feet)
- B. 36 metres (120 feet)
- C. 53 metres (175 feet)
- D. 96 metres (315 feet)

Your thinking distance in feet is approximately the same number as your speed in mph. At 40 mph your thinking distance is 40 ft. To find your braking distance in feet you multiply your speed in mph (40) by its first figure (4) and divide the result (40 x 4 = 160) by 2 (160 ÷ 2 = 80). Add your thinking distance (40 ft) to your braking distance (80 ft) to get your shortest overall stopping distance: 120 ft at 40 mph.

Q233 What is the braking distance at 50 mph?

Mark one answer
- A. 55 m (180 ft)
- B. 38 m (125 ft)
- C. 24 m (79 ft)
- D. 14 m (46 ft)

To find the braking distance in feet, multiply the speed in mph (50) by its first figure (5) and divide the result (50 x 5 = 250) by 2 (250 ÷ 2 = 125 ft).

Q234 You are driving at 50 mph in good conditions. What would be your shortest stopping distance?

Mark one answer
- A. 23 metres (75 feet)
- B. 36 metres (120 feet)
- C. 53 metres (175 feet)
- D. 73 metres (240 feet)

Thinking distance in feet is approximately the same number as the speed in mph. The shortest stopping distance at 50 mph = thinking distance (50 ft) + braking distance (125 ft).

Q235 You are travelling at 50 mph on a good dry road. What is your overall stopping distance?

Mark one answer
- A. 36 metres (120 feet)
- B. 53 metres (175 feet)
- C. 75 metres (245 feet)
- D. 96 metres (315 feet)

Remember that this is your shortest stopping distance as an alert, fit driver with a well-maintained car travelling in good conditions. Do not drive if you are unwell or your car is unroadworthy.

Q236 What is the shortest overall stopping distance on a dry road from 60 mph?

Mark one answer
- A. 53 metres (175 feet)
- B. 58 metres (190 feet)
- C. 73 metres (240 feet)
- D. 96 metres (315 feet)

Thinking distance = 60 ft. Braking distance is (60 x 6) ÷ 2 = 180 ft.
Shortest overall stopping distance = thinking distance + braking distance.

Q237 What is the shortest stopping distance at 70 mph?

Mark one answer
- A. 53 metres (175 feet)
- B. 60 metres (200 feet)
- C. 73 metres (240 feet)
- D. 96 metres (315 feet)

Thinking distance = 70 ft. Braking distance is (70 x 7) ÷ 2 = 245 ft.
Shortest overall stopping distance = thinking distance + braking distance.

Q238 **Your overall stopping distance will be much longer when driving**

Mark one answer
- **A.** In fog
- **B.** At night
- **C.** In the rain
- **D.** In strong winds

On wet roads your stopping distances will be at least double what they are on dry roads. Your speed has a bigger effect on your braking distance than on your thinking distance. If you halve your speed you will more than halve your overall stopping distance. Always drive more slowly at night and in adverse conditions such as fog.

Q239 **What is the main reason why your stopping distance is longer after heavy rain?**

Mark one answer
- **A.** The brakes will be cold because they are wet
- **B.** You may not be able to see large puddles
- **C.** Your tyres will have less grip on the road
- **D.** Water on the windscreen will blur your view of the road ahead

Water makes road surfaces slippery and greatly increases stopping distances. The tread pattern and depth are designed so your tyres can, for example, disperse up to 5 gallons of water per second and keep contact with the road at 60 mph. Driving too fast with worn tyres on wet roads can cause aquaplaning. The tyres ride up on the water, lose their grip and cause the vehicle to slide and skid.

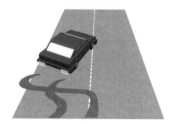

Q240 **You are braking on a wet road. Your vehicle begins to skid. What is the first thing you should do?**

Mark one answer
- **A.** Release the brake fully
- **B.** Push harder on the brake pedal
- **C.** Put your foot on the clutch
- **D.** Quickly pull up the handbrake

In any skid, take your foot off the brake immediately. Keep a light grip on the steering wheel with *both* hands and leave the car in gear. See **Q138** and **Q139**. Remember that it is better to avoid a skid in the first place.

Q241 You are turning left on a slippery road.
The back of your vehicle slides to the right.
What should you do?

Mark one answer

A. Brake firmly and do not turn the steering wheel

B. Steer carefully to the right

C. Turn only to the left

D. Use the clutch and brake firmly

In a rear wheel skid, steer left if the rear of the car is sliding to the left. Steer right if the rear of the car is sliding to the right. Do not oversteer. You could cause a skid in the opposite direction. In a front wheel skid, release your accelerator pedal immediately and wait for your front tyres to regain some grip before trying to steer.

Q242 You have driven through a flood. What is the first thing you should do?

Mark one answer

A. Stop and check the tyres

B. Stop and dry the brakes

C. Switch on your windscreen wipers

D. Test your brakes

Your brakes may fail if water gets on to the friction material of the drum linings or brake pads. Testing your brakes in wet conditions will help to dry them out and restore their efficiency. See **Q140**.

Q243 Braking distances on ice can be

Mark one answer

A. Twice normal distance

B. 5 times normal distance

C. 7 times normal distance

D. 10 times normal distance

Driving in snow and on ice is extremely dangerous. You face the constant risk of the wheels spinning or locking. Drive slowly in the highest gear possible. Steer smoothly. Use engine braking and try to avoid touching the brake pedal especially on corners.

Q244 Freezing conditions will affect the distance it takes you to come to a stop. You should expect stopping distances to increase by up to

Mark one answer
- A. 10 times
- B. 5 times
- C. 3 times
- D. 2 times

If you touch the brake pedal, you must do so extremely gently when driving on icy roads. The wheels can easily lock so that you lose control of your steering and begin to skid.

Q245 How can you tell when you are driving over black ice?

Mark one answer
- A. It would be easier to brake
- B. The noise from your tyres would sound louder
- C. You would see black ice on the road
- D. Your steering would feel light

One problem with 'black ice' is that you are usually unaware of it until your steering begins to feel light. If you are driving too fast for the conditions this warning comes too late. Do remember that it is better to avoid a skid than have to deal with one.

Q246 When driving in icy conditions the steering becomes light because the tyres

Mark one answer
- A. Are too hard
- B. Are too soft
- C. Have less grip on the road
- D. Have more grip on the road

Always keep your tyres inflated to the pressures recomended by the manufacturer. Do **not** lower the pressure for icy conditions. You will not improve their grip but you will increase the risk of damage to their walls.

Q247 You are driving in heavy rain when your steering suddenly becomes very light. To get control again you must

Mark one answer

A. Brake lightly to reduce speed
B. Change down to a lower gear
C. Ease off the accelerator
D. Steer towards a dry part of the road

You apply engine braking when you take your foot off the accelerator pedal. The lower the gear you are in the greater the engine braking. Easing off the accelerator is the first step in any progressive braking routine.

Q248 How can you avoid wheel spin when driving in freezing conditions?

Mark one answer

A. Allow the vehicle to coast in neutral
B. Drive in as high a gear as possible
C. Stay in first gear all the time
D. Put on your handbrake if the wheels begin to slip

The engine supplies the greatest power to the wheels when the vehicle is in its lowest gear. This is why you normally use the lowest gear when moving off and keep in a low gear when climbing hills. Less power is needed for driving at a constant speed on a level road so then you use a high gear. On icy roads you need gentle acceleration so the wheels turn slowly.

Q249 You are driving on an icy road. How can you avoid wheel spin?

Mark one answer

A. Brake gently and repeatedly
B. Drive in a low gear at all times
C. Drive at a slow speed in as high a gear possible
D. Use the hand brake if the wheels start to slip

On icy roads you want to avoid wheel spin and wheel lock. You risk wheel spin by harsh acceleration in low gear. You risk locking the wheels by harsh braking in any gear. Remember that you apply the handbrake to lock the rear brakes and only after you have stopped moving.

Q250 When driving in snow it is best to keep in as high a gear as possible. Why is this?

Mark one answer
- ○ **A.** So that wheel spin does not cause your engine to run too fast
- ○ **B.** To help to prevent wheel spin
- ○ **C.** To leave a lower gear available in case of wheel spin
- ○ **D.** To help you slow down quickly when you brake

See **Q248** and **Q249** above.

Q251 You are driving in freezing conditions. Which THREE should you do when approaching a sharp bend?

Mark three answers
- ○ **A.** Accelerate into the bend
- ○ **B.** Avoid sudden steering movements
- ○ **C.** Drive in as high a gear as you can
- ○ **D.** Gently apply your handbrake
- ○ **E.** Keep your clutch down throughout
- ○ **F.** Slow down before you reach the bend

On icy roads you must avoid sudden changes of speed and/or direction. Keep the clutch up. Take your foot off the accelerator to let engine braking gently slow your vehicle *before* you reach any bend or corner. Turn the steering wheel as smoothly as possible.

Q252 When driving in fog in daylight you should use

Mark one answer
- ○ **A.** Dipped headlights
- ○ **B.** Full-beam headlights
- ○ **C.** Hazard lights
- ○ **D.** Side lights

See **Q152** to **Q161** inclusive.

Q253 **What TWO safeguards could you take against fire risk to your vehicle?**

Mark two answers
- A. Avoid driving with a full tank of fuel
- B. Carry a fire extinguisher
- C. Check out any strong smell of petrol
- D. Keep water levels above maximum
- E. Use unleaded petrol
- F. Use a low octane fuel

There is always a serious fire risk and explosion if petrol or its vapour leaks out. When you are refuelling do not let your tank overflow. Stop refuelling when the trigger in the nozzle of the petrol pump cuts out automatically. In the event of a fire, keep people at a safe distance. Do **not** put water on to burning fuel. Use a dry powder or foam extinguisher. If you cannot control the fire at its outbreak, keep clear and wait for the fire brigade.

Q254 **You arrive at the scene of an accident involving a lorry carrying dangerous chemicals. What should you do before you dial 999?**

Mark one answer
- A. Find out about the chemicals from labels on the lorry
- B. Try to dilute the chemicals by washing them away with water
- C. Try to move the lorry
- D. Try to stop the chemicals spreading

The emergency services need to know how dangerous the chemicals are. An information panel on the lorry may tell them whether the chemicals are toxic, corrosive, flammable, radioactive, etc. A telephone number on the panel lets them call someone who can give them further information about the lorry and its load. You can find an illustration of a panel and some hazard symbols in The Highway Code.

Q255 **You arrive at the scene of a motorcycle accident. The rider is conscious but in shock. You should make sure that**

Mark one answer
- A. The rider's helmet is removed
- B. The rider's helmet is not removed
- C. The rider is moved to the side of the road
- D. The rider is put in the recovery position

You should remove the helmet only if the rider has stopped breathing and you cannot begin resuscitation if the helmet is left on. As soon as you have removed the helmet, clear the casualty's mouth of any obvious obstruction and tilt the head back. If breathing does not begin spontaneously, pinch the casualty's nose and blow into the mouth until the chest rises. Stop and repeat the procedure once every four seconds until the casualty can breath unaided.

Q256 You have stopped at the scene of an accident to give help. Which THREE things should you do?

Mark three answers

- ⬭ **A.** Give injured people a warm drink
- ⬭ **B.** Keep injured people on the move by walking them around
- ⬭ **C.** Keep injured people warm and comfortable
- ⬭ **D.** Keep injured people calm by talking to them reassuringly
- ⬭ **E.** Make sure injured people are not left alone

Never give casualties anything to drink. Never move casualties unless they are in danger. If you attempt to move a casualty you may make their injuries worse.

Q257 You are the first person to arrive at an accident where people are badly injured. Which THREE should you do?

Mark three answers

- ⬭ **A.** Get people who are not injured clear of the scene
- ⬭ **B.** Make sure someone telephones for an ambulance
- ⬭ **C.** Move the people who are injured clear of their vehicles
- ⬭ **D.** Switch on your own hazard warning lights
- ⬭ **E.** Give drinks to injured people

If you are the first to arrive at the scene of an accident, stop and switch on your hazard lights to warn others. Send for the emergency services. Set up a warning triangle. Switch off engines and stop anyone smoking. Try to minimise the risk of fire and further collisions. Do not move casualties unless they are in danger but get any uninjured people clear of the scene.

Q258 You are the first to arrive at the scene of an accident. Which FOUR of these should you do?

Mark four answers

- ⬭ **A.** Call the emergency services
- ⬭ **B.** Leave as soon as another motorist arrives
- ⬭ **C.** Move uninjured people away from the vehicles
- ⬭ **D.** Switch off the vehicle engines
- ⬭ **E.** Warn other traffic

You should not leave the scene of an accident until the emergency services have arrived and, if appropriate, you have given details to anyone with reasonable grounds for requiring them.

Q259 You are involved in an accident. A passenger in another vehicle is slightly injured. Do you have to report it to the police?

Mark one answer

◯ A. Yes, you must report it within 28 days
◯ B. No, slight injuries should not involve the police
◯ C. Yes, you must report it to the police as soon as possible
◯ D. No, the injured passenger should decide whether to report it

If you cannot report the accident to a police officer at the scene, you must report the accident to the police as soon as possible and in any case within 24 hours. If you cannot produce your insurance certificate at the time of the accident, you must take it to a police station within seven days. Always notify your insurance company of any accident even if you are not to blame and you are not making a claim.

Q260 You have an accident while driving and someone is injured. You must report it to the police as soon as possible, or within

Mark one answer

◯ A. 24 hours
◯ B. 48 hours
◯ C. 5 days
◯ D. 7 days

If no-one is hurt but you cause damage or you injure a dog, ass, mule, pig, goat, sheep, horse or cattle, you must give details to anyone with reasonably entitled to require. If you cannot do so, you must report the accident to the police as soon as possible and in any case within the same period required if someone had been injured.

Q261 You are in an accident on an "A" class road. At what distance before the obstruction should you place a warning triangle?

Mark one answer

◯ A. 25 metres (80 feet)
◯ B. 50 metres (165 feet)
◯ C. 100 metres (330 feet)
◯ D. 150 metres (495 feet)

Accidents usually cause an obstruction. Then there is the danger of other vehicles colliding into it. A triangle should warn traffic of danger ahead so there is enough time to take appropriate action.

Q262 Your vehicle is broken down on a straight road. Where should you place a warning triangle?

Mark one answer
- A. Directly at the rear of your vehicle
- B. Securely on the roof of your vehicle
- C. 10 metres (11 yards) from your vehicle
- D. 50 metres (55 yards) from your vehicle

If a warning triangle is placed too far away from an obstruction, it could mislead other drivers into thinking the triangle has been forgotten and there is no danger ahead.

Q263 You have broken down on a two-way road. You should place a warning triangle at least how far from your vehicle?

Mark one answer
- A. 5 metres (5 yards)
- B. 25 metres (27 yards)
- C. 50 metres (55 yards)
- D. 100 metres (110 yards)

If you break down on a motorway you should, if possible, place a warning triangle on the hard shoulder 150 metres (492 ft) back from your vehicle to alert other drivers. **Never** attempt to put a warning triangle on the carriageway.

Q264 You break down on an ordinary road. Your warning triangle should be displayed

Mark one answer
- A. At least 50 metres (55 yards) behind your vehicle
- B. At least 150 metres (164 yards) behind your vehicle
- C. Just behind your vehicle
- D. On the roof of your vehicle

Remember to place the triangle on the same side of road as the obstruction. This is usually on the left-hand side of the street and facing the traffic approaching your vehicle. Where should you put it if your vehicle has broken down in a one-way street?

Q265 **When are you allowed to use hazard warning lights?**

Mark one answer

- A. When driving during darkness without headlights
- B. When parked for shopping on double yellow lines
- C. When stopped and temporarily obstructing traffic
- D. When travelling slowly because you are lost

See **Q196 - Q199.** Hazard warning lights are for real emergencies only. Your vehicle must not be moving unless you are on a motorway or unrestricted dual carriageway and warning drivers behind you of danger ahead. Their use does not authorise you to park illegally or ignore parking restrictions.

Q266 **When should you switch on your hazard warning lights?**

Mark one answer

- A. When you are driving slowly due to bad weather
- B. When you are parked on double yellow lines
- C. When you are towing a broken down vehicle
- D. When you cannot avoid causing an obstruction

If your vehicle breaks down, get it off the road as soon as possible so that it does not obstruct other traffic. Get your vehicle onto the hard shoulder if you have a breakdown on the motorway.

Q267 **For which TWO should you use hazard warning lights?**

Mark two answers

- A. When you have broken down
- B. When you need to park on the pavement
- C. When you slow down quickly on a motorway because of a hazard ahead
- D. When you wish to stop on double yellow lines

You warn other road users of a hazard or a temporary obstruction when you switch on all four indicator lights to flash at the same time. It is an offence to use hazard warning lights other than in an emergency. See **Q196** to **Q199.**

Q268 For which THREE should you use your hazard warning lights?

Mark three answers

A. To warn following traffic of a hazard ahead

B. When you have broken down

C. When you are parking in a restricted area

D. When you are temporarily obstructing traffic

Q269 You are travelling on a motorway. A suitcase falls from your vehicle. There are valuables in the suitcase. What should you do?

Mark one answer

A. Reverse your vehicle carefully and collect the case as quickly as possible

B. Stop on the hard shoulder and then retrieve the suitcase yourself

C. Stop wherever you are and pick up the case but only when there is a safe gap

D. Stop on the hard shoulder and use the emergency telephone to inform the police

It is an offence to cause danger by carrying an insecure load. Luggage on your roof rack will increase fuel consumption and running costs. It may make your car less stable. If you overload the roof rack, your insurance company could refuse your claim for damage or loss. See **Q167**.

Q270 You are on the motorway. Luggage falls from your vehicle. What should you do?

Mark one answer

A. Pull up on the hard shoulder and wave traffic down

B. Reverse back up the motorway to pick it up

C. Stop at the next emergency telephone and contact the police

D. Stop on the motorway and put on hazard lights whilst you pick it up

Motorways are extremely dangerous places for stationary vehicles and pedestrians even on the hard shoulder. You will find a free-call telephone at one mile intervals along the hard shoulder so you can contact the emergency services.

Q271 You are driving on a motorway. A large box falls onto the carriageway from a lorry ahead of you. The lorry does not stop. You should

Mark one answer

⬭ **A.** Catch up with the lorry and try to get the driver's attention

⬭ **B.** Drive to the next emergency telephone and inform the police

⬭ **C.** Pull over to the hard shoulder then try and remove the box

⬭ **D.** Stop close to the box and switch on your hazard warning lights until the police arrive

If you have to stop because you cannot change lanes to avoid the box, you must switch on your hazard warning lights to alert traffic following behind you. Use your car telephone, if you have one, to contact the emergency services.

Q272 Your vehicle breaks down on a motorway. You go to the emergency telephone. Your passengers should

Mark one answer

⬭ **A.** Accompany you to the telephone

⬭ **B.** Stand next to the vehicle on the hard shoulder

⬭ **C.** Wait inside the vehicle

⬭ **D.** Wait on the embankment away from the hard shoulder

A stationary vehicle on the hard shoulder is always at risk from a collision even with its hazard warning lights flashing. You and your passengers should stand well clear. Children should be supervised and disabled passengers unable to get out should keep their seat belt on. See **Q357** to **Q362**.

Q273 Your vehicle has a puncture on a motorway. What should you do?

Mark one answer

⬭ **A.** Drive slowly to the next service area to get assistance

⬭ **B.** Pull up on the hard shoulder. Use the emergency phone to get assistance

⬭ **C.** Pull up on the hard shoulder. Change the wheel as quickly as possible

⬭ **D.** Switch on your hazard lights. Stop in your lane

Even if you have put up a warning triangle 150 m (492 ft) back on the hard shoulder and even if you are capable of changing a wheel yourself, you must call the emergency services. The police need to know your position in order to protect you and other motorway users. See **Q362**

Q274 Your tyre bursts while you are driving. Which TWO things should you do?

Mark two answers
- A. Give a stopping arm signal and use the gears to slow down
- B. Hold the steering wheel firmly to keep control
- C. Pull up slowly at the side of the road
- D. Select reverse gear to stop the vehicle
- E. Stop the vehicle by braking as quickly as possible

If a tyre bursts you will feel the steering become heavy. Your car may become difficult to control and tend to slew off the road when you brake. Remember it is an offence to drive on under-inflated tyres. And driving on a flat tyre even for a short distance can damage it beyond repair. Find a safe place and change the wheel as soon as possible.

Q275 Which TWO things should you do when a front tyre bursts?

Mark two answers
- A. Brake firmly and quickly
- B. Change down and brake hard
- C. Grip the steering wheel firmly
- D. Hold the steering wheel lightly
- E. Let the vehicle roll to a stop

If you press the brake pedal when a tyre bursts, you could lose control and slew off the road. You should take firm hold of the steering wheel with both hands to keep the vehicle under control. At the same time, keep off the accelerator and brake pedal so that engine braking can occur.

Q276 At a railway level crossing, the red light signal continues to flash after a train has gone by. What should you do?

Mark one answer
- A. Alert drivers behind you
- B. Phone the signal operator
- C. Proceed with caution
- D. Wait

Trains always have priority where the track crosses a road. A flashing red light signals the approach of one or more trains. You **MUST STOP** behind the white line in front of the barrier. Be a patient driver not a hospital patient.

Q277 You have stalled in the middle of a level crossing and cannot re-start the engine. The warning bell starts to ring. You should

Mark one answer

○ **A.** Carry on trying to re-start the engine
○ **B.** Get out and clear of the crossing
○ **C.** Push the vehicle clear of the crossing
○ **D.** Run down the track to warn the signalman

After the warning bell starts ringing, the barriers come down to keep the track clear for the trains about to arrive. In these circumstances, your first priority is get yourself clear of the crossing.

Q278 Your vehicle has broken down on an automatic railway level crossing. What should you do FIRST?

Mark one answer

○ **A.** Get everyone out of the vehicle and clear of the crossing
○ **B.** Phone the signal operator so that trains can be stopped
○ **C.** Try to push the vehicle clear of the crossing as soon as possible
○ **D.** Walk along the track to give warning to any approaching trains

Preventing injury to yourself and others should take priority over avoiding damage to property. When everyone is clear of the crossing, you should immediately contact the signal operator to warn of danger to the trains. Then follow any instructions the operator may give you.

Q279 You break down on a level crossing. The lights have not yet begun to flash. Which THREE things should you do?

Mark three answers

○ **A.** Leave your vehicle and get everyone clear
○ **B.** Move the vehicle if a signal operator tells you to
○ **C.** Telephone the signal operator
○ **D.** Tell drivers behind what has happened
○ **E.** Walk down the track and signal the next train

If you unavoidably break down on a crossing, take the following steps promptly and in order:
1. move yourself and others clear of the crossing
2. make telephone contact with the signal operator
3. follow any instructions the signal operator gives you.

The four topics in this section are about **motoring regulations** and **laws**. The first topic is about documents required for using vehicles. The next two topics are about regulations for roads and motorways. The fourth topic deals with traffic signs, road markings, signals, speed limits, priority and rights of way.

DOCUMENTS

By law you require a *driving licence* (signed and valid for your vehicle), a *vehicle excise licence* (current tax disc displayed on the vehicle) and *third party insurance* (against liability for damage to property and injury to other people including passengers). Driving without this minimum insurance is a very serious offence. You are not required by law to carry insurance for fire, theft or personal injury even though many sensible people do. If your motor car is over three years old you also require a current *test certificate* (MOT).

RULES OF THE ROAD

Speed Limits

A speed limit is a maximum, **not** a target. Speed limits depend on the type of road and the type of vehicle. 30 mph is normal in built up areas. When there are no street lamps at frequent intervals, speed limit signs are displayed. Remember that speeds under 30 mph may still be too fast for many road and traffic conditions. 40 mph limits often apply near the edges of towns and on dual carriageways where repeater speed limit signs are displayed and traffic may flow faster. Good drivers try to keep up with the flow of traffic but without breaking the speed limit.

60 mph is the national speed limit for single carriageway roads. When it applies in rural areas there are usually no signs or street lamps. When the national speed limit applies in urban areas there are repeater signs displayed. 70 mph is the maximum speed limit on dual carriageways. When the limit on a rural road or a dual carriageway is restricted to 50 mph, watch out for additional hazards such as dangerous junctions, unexpected traffic lights and pedestrians crossing.

Parking and lighting

We do **not** have an automatic right to park on the roads. By law they are 'for the purpose of passage'. To keep within the law we should either get permission from a uniformed police officer (or traffic warden) or use an authorised parking place such as a parking meter bay. If you park in an unauthorised place you could be charged with dangerous parking, obstruction and other illegal parking offences. You are causing an obstruction if you park your car on a pavement or grass verge. Leaving your car on the wrong side of the road after dark is dangerous parking. Check The Highway Code for details on parking regulations, but in general the rules are quite clear:

Never park your vehicle where it could be a danger or inconvenience to pedestrians and other road users

MOTORWAY RULES

The maximum speed limit on motorways is 70 mph for motorcycles, cars, buses and coaches. It is 60 mph for articulated goods vehicles, those towing a trailer or those exceeding 7.5 tonnes. The maximum speed limit is also 60 mph if your car is towing a caravan or trailer.

Motorway traffic is one-way. You must never reverse, drive against the traffic flow or cross the central reservation. Keep in the left lane. Overtake only on the right unless traffic is moving slowly in queues. Do not use the right-hand lane of a three-lane motorway if your vehicle is towing a caravan or trailer. You must not stop on the motorway (and slipways) except in an emergency and then only on the hard shoulder. Being in need of sleep is **not** an emergency according to the law.

ROAD AND TRAFFIC SIGNS

Signals, signs and road markings all help to keep traffic flowing safely but only if you see and act upon them correctly.

Always obey The Highway Code

Traffic signs
You need to understand the basic shapes and diagrams on the signs. The colours are not essential but they do make the signs clearer. The red STOP sign has the octagon shape and means you must stop at the line. The GIVE WAY sign has the upside down triangle shape. It warns you to be prepared to stop at the STOP sign or to give way at the GIVE WAY sign. Both signs are extremely important and easily recognised. Other signs giving orders are mostly circular. Blue means a positive order (**do**). Red means a negative order (**don't**). Warning signs are mostly triangles with a red border. You should heed the warning even though you need not obey the sign. Information and direction signs are rectangular with a blue background for motorway signs and a green background for primary route signs.

Road markings
White lines along the middle of the road separate traffic travelling in opposite directions and warn you of additional danger. More white paint means more danger. There are restrictions on parking, stopping and waiting alongside double white lines even if one is broken.

Do not straddle or cross
- a single broken line, with long markings and short gaps, unless you can see that the road is clear well ahead
- a double white line except from the broken line side and unless it is safe to do so
- a **double solid** white line from either direction except in an emergency

It is extremely dangerous to cross a double white line but you may do so to get in and out of premises, to avoid a stationary obstruction or to turn into a side road. It is illegal to straddle or cross a double solid white line in order to overtake an obstruction travelling at less than 10 mph unless it is a horse and rider, a pedal cyclist or a road maintenance vehicle. Note that slow moving tractors are **not** road maintenance vehicles!

There are parking restrictions by yellow lines at the roadside and loading/unloading restrictions by yellow lines on the kerb. More yellow paint means less parking and waiting because there is more danger. Zigzag markings warn you of the special dangers at pedestrian crossings and school entrances where you must not stop to load or unload goods or passengers. Parking, stopping and waiting regulations apply alongside double white lines even if one is broken and even without yellow lines at the kerbside.

> **Always park in the safest place to avoid creating danger and problems for others.**

Traffic lights
You must know the sequence of the signals at traffic lights and pedestrian crossings. Red means stop. Green means go *only if the way forward is clear* so you must take care when approaching a green light. The amber light means stop. Never cross it except in the emergency of avoiding an accident with another vehicle.

Signals by authorised persons
Uniformed police officers are authorised to control traffic. They use their right arm to signal to traffic approaching them from the front. Their left arm is for traffic coming from behind. They keep their arms still to stop the traffic. They move their arms to wave traffic on. A police officer's signals can override any other traffic controls and must be obeyed. Traffic wardens have the same authority as police to control traffic and use the same arm signals. School Crossing Patrols are authorised to assist children crossing roads on their way to and from schools. You must stop your vehicle when a crossing patrol shows you the Stop – Children sign. Traffic signs operated by workmen have the same meanings as any other traffic lights. A person in charge of animals is also allowed to control traffic. If a traffic controller directs you to cross a hazard warning line, it is still your responsibility to do so safely.

Q280 To drive on the road learners MUST

Mark one answer
- ○ **A.** Apply for a driving test within 12 months
- ○ **B.** Have NO penalty points on their licence
- ○ **C.** Have a signed, valid provisional licence
- ○ **D.** Have taken professional instruction

When you receive your licence, you should check the details and sign it. If you do not sign your licence it will not be valid. When you have completed your course of professional instruction and passed your test, the same will apply to the full driving licence you are granted. Remember that you must also be medically fit to drive. An undisclosed disability could invalidate your licence.

Q281 Who MUST you show your driving licence to, on demand?

Mark one answer
- ○ **A.** A third party after an accident
- ○ **B.** A traffic warden
- ○ **C.** A uniformed police officer
- ○ **D.** A vehicle inspector

You may find your licence accepted by people in various organisations who require some form of identification. By law, however, you are only required to show your licence to a police officer in uniform when it is requested. At an accident you must provide your name, address and other details to anyone having reasonable grounds for requiring them.

Q282 Which THREE of the following do you need before you can drive legally?

Mark three answers
- ○ **A.** A current MOT certificate if the car is over 3 years old
- ○ **B.** Fully comprehensive insurance
- ○ **C.** Proof of your identity
- ○ **D.** A signed driving licence
- ○ **E.** A valid tax disk displayed on your vehicle
- ○ **F.** A vehicle handbook

You must display a valid tax disk as proof that you have paid your vehicle excise licence fee. Remember that a current MOT certificate is no guarantee that your vehicle is in a roadworthy condition. Always do your routine daily and weekly checks. Be sure your vehicle is serviced properly and regularly.

Q283 Before driving anyone else's motor vehicle you should make sure that

Mark one answer
- A. The owner has left the insurance documents in the vehicle
- B. The vehicle owner has third party insurance cover
- C. The vehicle is insured for your use
- D. Your own vehicle has insurance cover

You must never drive a vehicle unless it is insured for you to use. Driving without insurance is a serious offence which could lead to possible disqualification and a fine of up to £5000. Your own car insurance may cover you to drive other cars. Remember that your insurance for other cars may be third party only. It may not cover damage to any other car you are driving even if it gives comprehensive cover for your own car.

Q284 What is the legal minimum insurance cover you must have to drive on public roads?

Mark one answer
- A. Fully comprehensive
- B. Personal injury cover
- C. Third party, fire and theft
- D. Third party only

By law, your vehicle must be properly insured to cover against third party and passenger liability. This means your vehicle is insured against any claim by passengers or other persons for damage or injury to their person or property. It usually costs very little more for Third Party, Fire & Theft insurance to cover your own vehicle against damage by fire and loss by theft.

Q285 For which TWO of these must you show your motor insurance certificate?

Mark two answers
- A. When buying or selling a vehicle
- B. When having an M.O.T. inspection
- C. When a police officer asks you for them
- D. When you are taking your driving test
- E. When you are taxing your vehicle

You cannot tax a vehicle that is uninsured. Driving without insurance is a very serious offence that the DVLA cannot condone. If you are involved in an accident causing injury, you will be required to show the police your valid motor insurance certificate.

Q286 Motorcars and motorcycles must FIRST have an MOT test certificate when they are

Mark one answer
- A. One year old
- B. Three years old
- C. Five years old
- D. Seven years old

An MOT certificate relates only to the condition of the items examined on the day of the test. It does not cover the condition of the engine, clutch or gearbox. The certificate is valid for 12 months but does not confirm that the vehicle will remain roadworthy for that period of time. You can apply for a new certificate not more than one month before the old one expires. If you produce your old certificate when your new one is being issued, the new expiry date may be entered as 12 months from the expiry date of the old certificate.

Q287 When is it legal to drive a car over 3 years old without an MOT certificate?

Mark one answer
- A. Just after buying a second-hand car with no MOT
- B. Up to 7 days after the old certificate has run out
- C. When driving to an appointment at an MOT centre
- D. When driving to an MOT centre to arrange an appointment

It is an offence to drive a car that is not roadworthy. It is also an offence to drive a roadworthy car without a valid MOT certificate if that car is more than 3 years old. The only exception is when driving to an authorised MOT test centre for an examination booked in advance.

Q288 A police officer asks to see your driving documents. You don't have them with you. You may produce them at a police station within

Mark one answer
- A. 5 days
- B. 7 days
- C. 14 days
- D. 21 days

It may be convenient to carry around your motor insurance certificate with your driving licence. It may not be wise or safe ever to leave the certificate in your vehicle.

Q289 **Which THREE pieces of information are found on a vehicle registration document?**

Mark three answers
- A. Date of MOT
- B. Engine size
- C. Make of vehicle
- D. Registered keeper
- E. Service history details
- F. Type of insurance cover

You should keep your vehicle registration document in a safe place – **NEVER IN THE VEHICLE**. You are required by law to notify the DVLA (Driver and Vehicle Licensing Authority) of any changes to the name and address or vehicle particulars printed on the document as soon as they occur. It is an offence to alter or obliterate any details in the document or to supply false information for the purpose of registration.

Q290 **What should you bring with you when taking your driving test?**

Mark one answer
- A. An insurance certificate
- B. An M.O.T. certificate
- C. A service record book
- D. A signed driving licence

The driving examiner will regard your signed valid driving licence as proof of your identity. Do not let anyone else have it. If you forget your licence, the examiner will require some other acceptable form of identity such as your passport.

Q291 **Select TWO answers. To supervise a learner driver you MUST**

Mark two answers
- A. Be at least 21
- B. Be an approved driving instructor
- C. Hold an advanced driving certificate
- D. Have held a full licence for at least 3 years

There is no substitute for proper lessons from a fully qualified driving approved by the Department of Transport. There is also no substitute for good experience gained through proper practice. Anyone supervising learner drivers must hold a full UK licence valid for the category of vehicle being driven by the learner. Your instructor should arrange for any would-be supervising relative or friend to attend one of your lessons. The instructor can make both of you aware of the legal responsibilities and conditions that apply to you and to anyone supervising you. You should encourage any relative or friend to take a refresher course in driving before they attempt to supervise your driving practice.

Q292 **In which TWO places must you NOT park?**

Mark two answers
- **A.** At a bus stop
- **B.** In a side-road
- **C.** In a one-way street
- **D.** Near a police station
- **E.** Near a school entrance

When you park on a road your vehicle restricts the width of road available to other traffic. It is also an obstruction which can hide pedestrians from the view of oncoming drivers. If you park near a bus stop you may add to the bus driver's difficulties in manoeuvring a large vehicle. If you park near a school you may make it more difficult for children to cross the road safely.

Q293 **In which THREE places must you NEVER park your vehicle?**

Mark three answers
- **A.** At or near a bus stop
- **B.** Near the brow of a hill
- **C.** On a 40 mph road
- **D.** Opposite hazard warning lines
- **E.** Within 10 metres of a junction

Around 75% of all accidents occur on built-up roads. More than two-thirds of these occur at or near junctions. Turning out of a junction can be difficult and dangerous. Vehicles parked close to the junction can make it even more difficult and dangerous. The vehicles may seriously restrict the width of road and the view available to road users. You must not park opposite double white hazard warning lines, even if one of them is a broken line.

Q294 **In which FOUR places must you NOT park or wait?**

Mark four answers
- **A.** At a bus stop
- **B.** In front of someone else's drive
- **C.** On a dual carriageway
- **D.** On the brow of a hill
- **E.** On the slope of a hill
- **F.** Opposite a traffic island

Always think carefully about where to stop, wait or park. Do not obstruct the passage of other road users especially if they are put at risk trying to avoid your vehicle. Traffic islands are often safe places in the road for pedestrians waiting to use a crossing. Remember that it is an offence to park within the area marked by the zigzag lines of a crossing.

Q295 At which of these places are you sometimes allowed to park your vehicle?

Mark one answer
- ○ **A.** On a clearway
- ○ **B.** On the nearside lane of a motorway
- ○ **C.** On the zigzag lines of a zebra crossing
- ○ **D.** Where there is a single broken yellow line

Always check the small print on the restriction plates and parking notices when yellow line parking restrictions are in force. It is also sensible to find, if possible, the particular reasons for any restrictions. Continuous single or double yellow lines warn you of severe restrictions on parking and waiting.

Q296 What MUST you have to park in a disabled space?

Mark one answer
- ○ **A.** An advanced driver certificate
- ○ **B.** A modified vehicle
- ○ **C.** An orange badge
- ○ **D.** A wheelchair

The local authority usually issue the parking permits for disabled drivers (or passengers) to use in the area where they normally live. Different local councils and city authorities have their own special rules. The official permit must be displayed like the tax disc in the windscreen. You should not confuse it with the disabled person stickers you sometimes see in car rear windows!

Q297 What is the nearest you may park your vehicle to a junction?

Mark one answer
- ○ **A.** 10 m (33 feet)
- ○ **B.** 12 m (40 feet)
- ○ **C.** 15 m (50 feet)
- ○ **D.** 20 m (65 feet)

Do not park closer to a junction than the legally required minimum distance unless you are occupying an authorised parking space. Parking any closer obscures the line of vision of other road users and makes it difficult for large trucks to turn into and out of the junction.

Q298 You are leaving your vehicle parked on a road. When may you leave the engine running?

Mark one answer

A. If the battery is flat
B. If you will be parked for less than five minutes
C. If there is a passenger in the vehicle
D. Not on any occasion

When you stop to park, always apply the handbrake, switch off the engine and switch off the headlights. On hills you should leave your vehicle in an appropriate gear. At night you may have to leave on your sidelights or parking lights. If your car is stolen when you leave it with the engine running, your insurance company may legally refuse to settle your claim against theft or related damages.

Q299 Your vehicle is parked on the road at night. When must you use side lights?

Mark one answer

A. Where you are near a bus stop
B. Where you are facing oncoming traffic
C. Where the speed limit exceeds 30 mph
D. Where there are continuous white lines in the middle of the road

When you park at night the headlights of oncoming traffic should cause your rear reflectors to give the drivers a red warning signal. Do not park alongside continuous white lines or near a bus stop.

Q300 You are parked in a busy high street. What is the safest way to turn your vehicle around to go the opposite way?

Mark one answer

A. Do a U-turn
B. Drive into a side-road and reverse into the main road
C. Find a quiet side-road to turn round in
D. Get someone to stop the traffic

In a busy street a U-turn would be highly dangerous if only because it involves cutting across at least two streams of traffic with one flowing in the opposite direction to the other. Reversing from a side-road into a main road is not permitted because it is extremely dangerous. Don't expect a uniformed police officer or traffic warden to hold up traffic just for your sake. In a quiet side-road or at the end of a cul-de-sac you can often find a safe and convenient turning circle.

Q301 **When may you reverse from a side-road into a main road?**

Mark one answer
- **A.** At any time
- **B.** NOT at any time
- **C.** Only if the main road is clear of traffic
- **D.** Only if both roads are clear of traffic

Just driving forwards from a side-road into a main road needs care. Parked vehicles may add to your difficulties by obscuring your view of the main road and traffic requiring priority. It would be foolish as well as illegal to reverse out of a side-road into a main road and its traffic.

Q302 **You MUST NOT reverse**

Mark one answer
- **A.** For more than a car's length
- **B.** For longer than necessary
- **C.** In a built-up area
- **D.** Into a side-road

You are allowed to reverse for more than a car's length in a built-up area and even in a one-way street, but only as part of your manoeuvre to park your vehicle parallel to the kerb. You may also reverse into a side-road to the left or right and to continue reversing until you are at least 10 metres back from the junction. In any event, however, you must never reverse for longer than necessary.

Q303 **You are on a busy main road and find you are travelling in the wrong direction. What should you do?**

Mark one answer
- **A.** Make a "three point" turn in the main road
- **B.** Make a U-turn in the main road
- **C.** Turn round in a side-road
- **D.** Turn into a side-road on the right and reverse into the main road

Never do anything that could increase the risks of an accident or force other road users to alter their speed and/or direction. A driving examiner would regard such an action as a fault. It could cause you to fail your test.

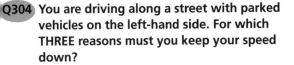

Q304 You are driving along a street with parked vehicles on the left-hand side. For which THREE reasons must you keep your speed down?

Mark three answers

A. Children may run out from between the vehicles

B. Drivers' doors may open

C. So that oncoming traffic can see you more clearly

D. Vehicles may be pulling out

E. You may set off car alarms

Always be alert for **moving hazards**: car doors opening suddenly, vehicles moving off without indicating, young children running into the road, elderly people stepping off the pavement, etc. See **Q10** and **Q11**.

Q305 You meet an obstruction on your side of the road. You must

Mark one answer

A. Accelerate to get past first

B. Drive on, it is your right of way

C. Give way to oncoming traffic

D. Wave oncoming vehicles through

Unless a road sign indicates otherwise you should give priority to oncoming traffic on the opposite side of the road. Try always to select and follow a smooth safety line that will take you past any obstruction on your side of the road. Hold back but stay on your safety line if you have to give priority to oncoming vehicles. Make eye contact with the drivers but do not flash your lights or wave them on. It is up to them to decide that you have held back and that it is safe for them to proceed.

Q306 As a car driver, which THREE lanes must you NOT use?

Mark three answers

A. Acceleration lane

B. Bus lane at the times shown

C. Crawler lane

D. Cycle lane

E. Overtaking lane

F. Tram lane

Take care not to obstruct buses and trams whose drivers have a timetable to follow. And take care not to endanger cyclists by driving close to or into their lane.

Q307 **Where may you overtake on a one-way street?**

Mark one answer
- A. Either on the right or the left
- B. Only on the left hand side
- C. Only on the right hand side
- D. Overtaking is not allowed

If you plan to turn at the end of a one-way street, you are permitted to overtake on the left to turn left and to overtake on the right to turn right. Signal and move into the appropriate lane in good time. Watch out for traffic changing lanes without warning at the last moment. See **Q6, Q131**.

Q308 **When going straight ahead at a roundabout, you should**

Mark one answer
- A. Indicate before leaving the roundabout
- B. Indicate right when approaching the roundabout
- C. Indicate left when approaching the roundabout
- D. Not indicate at any time

Roundabouts are circular one-way streets. You join on the left usually at give-way lines, not stop lines. You have a clear all-round view of oncoming traffic. You give priority to traffic already on the roundabout to your right. You merge without causing other vehicles to change speed and/or direction. You leave by an exit on your left.

Remember that the regulations for roundabouts apply in exactly the same way at mini-roundabouts.

Q309 **You are going straight ahead at a roundabout. How should you signal?**

Mark one answer

○ **A.** Signal left as you leave the exit off the roundabout

○ **B.** Signal left as you pass the exit before the one you will take

○ **C.** Signal left on the approach to the roundabout and keep the signal on until you leave

○ **D.** Signal right on the approach and then left to leave the roundabout

As you approach a roundabout, get into the most appropriate lane for your exit. This is usually the left lane for turning left or going straight ahead or the right lane for turning right. Slow down. Unless road markings indicate otherwise, give way to traffic already on the roundabout and coming from the right.

TO TURN LEFT:
1 Signal left on approach,
2 Keep to the left on the roundabout,
3 Keep signalling until you have taken your exit off the roundabout.

TO GO STRAIGHT AHEAD:
1 Do **not** signal on approach,
2 Keep in the lane you used to join the round-about,
3 Signal left just as you pass the exit before the one you want.

TO TURN RIGHT:
1 Signal right on approach,
2 Keep to the right on the roundabout and keep signalling right,
3 Signal left just as you pass the exit before the one you want.

When leaving the roundabout, watch out especially for two-wheeled vehicles. When you have left the roundabout, cancel your signal. Apply the same rules to mini-roundabouts.

Q310 **At a crossroads there are no signs or road markings. Two vehicles approach. Which has priority?**

Mark one answer

- A. The vehicle travelling the fastest
- B. The vehicle on the widest road
- C. Neither vehicle
- D. Vehicles approaching from the right

Take great care at unmarked crossroads. Make eye contact with drivers of other vehicles waiting at or just approaching the crossroads. Be prepared not only to give them priority but also to accept priority if appropriate and offered. Do **not** flash your lights, sound your horn or wave other road users on.

Q311 **Who has priority at an unmarked crossroads?**

Mark one answer

- A. No one
- B. The driver of the larger vehicle
- C. The driver who is going faster
- D. The driver on the wider road

Who actually gives or takes priority at unmarked crossroads can depend not only upon the skill and experience of the drivers but also upon the size and manoeuvrability of their vehicles. A small car might hold back or might go forward quickly to give a large vehicle room to turn.

Q312 **You are intending to turn RIGHT at a junction. An oncoming driver is also turning right. It will normally be safer to**

Mark one answer

- A. Carry on and turn at the next junction instead
- B. Hold back and wait for the other driver to turn first
- C. Keep the other vehicle to your RIGHT and turn behind it (offside-to-offside)
- D. Keep the other vehicle to your LEFT and turn in front of it (nearside-to-nearside)

When traffic or a junction layout makes you pass nearside-to-nearside, watch out for oncoming vehicles hidden from view. This is a major hazard especially with buses and other large vehicles that usually make offside-to-offside passing impossible.

Q313 When may you enter a box junction?

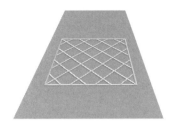

Mark one answer

- A. Only when your exit road is clear
- B. Only when there are less than two vehicles in front of you
- C. Whenever the traffic lights show green
- D. Whenever you need to turn right

A golden rule of driving: **do not proceed unless your way forward is clear**. This rule always applies and to every situation not just crossings, crossroads and junctions. You **must not** enter a yellow box junction until your exit road or lane is clear. But you may enter if you are only stopped from turning right by oncoming traffic or by vehicles turning right. See **Q22**.

Q314 At a pelican crossing, what does a flashing amber light mean?

Mark one answer

- A. You can move off, even if pedestrians are still on the crossing
- B. You must give way to pedestrians still on the crossing
- C. You must not move off until the lights stop flashing
- D. You must stop because the lights are about to change to red

Flashing amber lights warn of danger. You should be prepared to stop when you see them. You may also meet flashing amber lights on motorways and road maintenance vehicles as well as at railway and school crossings. See **Q15**.

Q315 On which THREE occasions MUST you stop your vehicle?

Mark three answers

- A. At a red traffic light
- B. At a junction with double broken white lines
- C. At a pelican crossing when the amber light is flashing and no pedestrians are crossing
- D. When involved in an accident
- E. When signalled to do so by a police officer

Double broken white lines across part of the road tell you to give-way. An unbroken white line means stop. Double broken white lines across the whole road tell signify a give-way junction at the end of a one-way street.

Q316 You MUST stop when signalled to do so by which THREE of these?

Mark three answers
- ○ **A.** A bus driver
- ○ **B.** A pedestrian
- ○ **C.** A police officer
- ○ **D.** A red traffic light
- ○ **E.** A school crossing patrol

If an unauthorised person signals you to stop, you need not stop but you should take care. There may be a good reason for the signal. You must stop at the scene of an accident unless a uniformed police officer or traffic warden directs you otherwise.

Q317 You see this sign ahead of you. It means

Mark one answer
- ○ **A.** Do not exceed 30 mph after passing it
- ○ **B.** The minimum speed limit ahead is 30 mph
- ○ **C.** Start to slow down to 30 mph after passing the sign
- ○ **D.** You are leaving the 30 mph speed limit area

Remember that a **maximum** speed limit is the **highest** speed you are allowed. It is **not** a target you must achieve. On many occasions and in many circumstances you must drive well below the speed limit to be safe.

Q318 If you see a 30 mph limit ahead, this means

Mark one answer
- ○ **A.** It is a guide. You are allowed to drive 10% faster
- ○ **B.** The restriction applies only during the working day
- ○ **C.** You must not exceed this speed
- ○ **D.** You must keep your speed up to 30 mph

It is an offence to break the speed limit. If you drive 10% faster than the speed limit you would still be breaking the law. It would be no defence to blame your speedometer for being only 90% accurate.

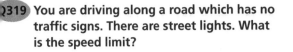

Q319 You are driving along a road which has no traffic signs. There are street lights. What is the speed limit?

Mark one answer

⭘ **A.** 20 mph
⭘ **B.** 30 mph
⭘ **C.** 40 mph
⭘ **D.** 60 mph

Q320 Where you see street lights but no speed limit signs, the limit is usually

Mark one answer

⭘ **A.** 30 mph
⭘ **B.** 40 mph
⭘ **C.** 50 mph
⭘ **D.** 60 mph

Q321 There are no speed limit signs on the road. How is a 30 mph limit indicated?

Mark one answer

⭘ **A.** By hazard warning lines
⭘ **B.** By pedestrian islands
⭘ **C.** By street lighting
⭘ **D.** By double or single yellow lines

A speed limit is determined by the national speed limit and by the class or type of the road and vehicle. The speed limit on a restricted road is 30 mph unless otherwise indicated. A road is restricted when there is street lighting not more than 200 yards apart. You should see speed limit and repeater signs displayed if a road without street lighting is classed as restricted or one with street lighting is classed as derestricted.

Q322 **What does a speed limit sign like this mean?**

Mark one answer
- **A.** It is safe to drive at the speed shown
- **B.** The speed shown is the advised maximum
- **C.** The speed shown allows for various road and weather conditions
- **D.** You must not exceed the speed shown

Remember: **circle = must** and **red = must not**. A minimum speed limit sign means you **must not** exceed that speed.

Q323 **What is the national speed limit for cars and motorcycles on a dual carriageway?**

Mark one answer
- **A.** 30 mph
- **B.** 50 mph
- **C.** 60 mph
- **D.** 70 mph

New learner drivers are not allowed to drive on motorways. They are allowed to drive on dual carriageways where they can gain valuable experience of some but not all the problems and responsibilities of motorway-style driving.

Q324 **You are driving in the right lane of a dual carriageway. You see signs showing that the right lane is closed 800 yards ahead. You should**

Mark one answer
- **A.** Keep in that lane until you reach the queue
- **B.** Move to the left immediately
- **C.** Move to the left in good time
- **D.** Wait and see which lane is moving faster

The higher your speed the further ahead you should look and plan your driving. Good drivers make allowances for drivers changing lanes at the last minute because of bad planning or inconsiderate driving. See **Q354.**

Q325 You are driving on a two-lane dual carriageway. For which TWO of these would you use the right-hand lane?

Mark two answers
- A. Constant high-speed driving
- B. Driving at the minimum allowed speed
- C. Normal driving
- D. Mending punctures
- E. Overtaking slower traffic
- F. Turning right

In the UK the general rule of the road is: drive on the left keeping to the left. For dual carriageways and motorways the general rule is: drive in the left lane except when overtaking slower moving traffic.

Q326 On a three-lane dual carriageway the right-hand lane can be used for

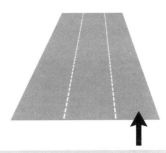

Mark one answer
- A. Fast moving traffic only
- B. Overtaking or turning right
- C. Overtaking only, never turning right
- D. Turning right only, never overtaking

On many dual carriageways you may turn right. This may be one of the reasons why dual carriageways are not so safe as motorways. **Never** call or think of the right lanes as the fast lanes. The speed limit applies equally to all lanes.

Q327 You are going along a single track road with passing places only on the right. The driver behind wishes to overtake. You should

Mark one answer
- A. Drive into a passing place on your right
- B. Speed up to get away from the following driver
- C. Switch on your hazard warning lights
- D. Wait opposite a passing place on your right

Q328 You are on a road which is only wide enough for one vehicle. There is a car coming towards you. Which TWO of these would be correct?

Mark two answers

- A. Force the other driver to reverse
- B. Pull into a passing place on your right
- C. Pull into a passing place on your left
- D. Pull into a passing place if your vehicle is wider
- E. Wait opposite a passing place on your right
- F. Wait opposite a passing place on your left

Places are usually available at intervals on single track roads to allow vehicles to pass one another. Never treat one as lay-by. If another vehicle wishes to pass you from whichever direction, pull into a passing place on your left or stop opposite a passing place on your right. In general you should give way to uphill traffic and to vehicles much larger than your own. See **Q134** and **Q135**.

Q329 You are driving over a level crossing. The warning lights come on and a bell rings. What should you do?

Mark one answer

- A. Get everyone out of the vehicle immediately
- B. Keep going and clear the crossing
- C. Stop and reverse back to clear the crossing
- D. Stop immediately and use your hazard warning lights

At railway crossings, the first warning of trains coming is bell and a steady amber light which means stop. This warning is followed by pairs of red lights starting to flash and the barriers coming down. You should keep going if you have already crossed the white line when the amber light comes on. But you *must not* cross the line when the red lights are flashing even if a train has gone by. It is only safe to cross when the lights go off and the barriers open. See **Q23**.

Q330 You are waiting at a level crossing. The red warning lights continue to flash after a train has passed by. What should you do?

Mark one answer

○ **A.** Continue to wait
○ **B.** Drive across carefully
○ **C.** Get out and investigate
○ **D.** Telephone the signal operator

At a railway level crossing, be patient and prepared to wait for more trains. A flashing red light signals the approach of trains which always have priority where the track crosses a road. Remain behind the white line in front of the barrier. Do not drive forward until the alarm and flashing lights are off and the barriers fully up. See **Q276 to Q279**

Q331 You are waiting at a level crossing. A train has passed but the lights keep flashing. You must

Mark one answer

○ **A.** Carry on waiting
○ **B.** Edge over the 'STOP' line and look for trains
○ **C.** Park your vehicle and investigate
○ **D.** Phone the signal operator

Q332 **Which of the following CAN travel on a motorway?**

Mark one answer
- ○ **A.** Cyclists
- ○ **B.** Learner drivers
- ○ **C.** Tractors
- ○ **D.** Vans

Motorways provide safe routes for full licence holders driving or riding vehicles capable of travelling at speeds up to 70 mph. They are not available to riders of mopeds or to new learner drivers.

Q333 **Which FOUR of these must not use motorways?**

Mark four answers
- ○ **A.** Cyclists
- ○ **B.** Double decker buses
- ○ **C.** Farm tractors
- ○ **D.** Horse riders
- ○ **E.** Learner car drivers
- ○ **F.** Motorcycles over 50cc

Dual carriageways may be used by agricultural vehicles, horse riders, cyclists and new learner drivers. The national speed limit applies unless a lower limit is otherwise indicated. This can put road users like cyclists and horse riders at serious risk from vehicles that might pass close by at their maximum permitted speed.

Q334 **You are joining a motorway from a slip road. You should**

Mark one answer
- ○ **A.** Match the speed of the traffic and move into a clear space
- ○ **B.** Wait at the beginning of the slip road for the traffic to clear
- ○ **C.** Wait at the end of the slip road for a safe gap
- ○ **D.** Wait for a vehicle in the nearest lane to move over

Slip roads are designed to let drivers adjust their speed so they can merge into a safe gap in the traffic already on the motorway. At some junctions signs may indicate that the slip road continues as an extra lane to become part of the motorway. Always give way to traffic already on the motorway. Do not leave the left lane to overtake until you have become accustomed to the speed of the motorway traffic.

Q335 You are joining a motorway. Why is it important to make full use of the slip road?

Mark one answer
- A. Because you can continue on the hard shoulder
- B. Because there is space available to slow down if you need to
- C. To build up a speed similar to traffic on the motorway
- D. To allow you direct access to the overtaking lanes

The slip road serves mainly as an acceleration lane. Traffic already on the motorway should assist vehicles using the slip road by keeping their own speed steady and, if safe and convenient, make a gap by moving out of the left lane.

Q336 When joining a motorway you must

Mark one answer
- A. Always give way to traffic already on the motorway
- B. Always use the hard shoulder
- C. Come to a stop before joining the motorway
- D. Stop at the end of the acceleration lane

Traffic may sometimes be directed to drive on the hard shoulder when motorway roadworks are in progress. At all other times you must use the hard shoulder only if you have to stop in an emergency. See **Q272** and **Q273**.

Q337 You are driving a car on a motorway. Unless signs show otherwise, you must NOT exceed

Mark one answer
- A. 80 mph
- B. 70 mph
- C. 60 mph
- D. 50 mph

Do not be tempted to break the law in response to other drivers exceeding the speed limit. Keep at least a two-second gap from the vehicle in front. Remember to increase it if road and weather conditions deteriorate.

Q338 What is the national speed limit on
motorways for cars and motorcycles?

Mark one answer
- A. 30 mph
- B. 50 mph
- C. 60 mph
- D. 70 mph

The national speed limits vary with the class of road and the type of vehicle. On motorways the speed limit for a car towing a caravan or trailer is the same as that for goods vehicles exceeding 7.5 tonnes maximum laden weight.

Q339 You are towing a trailer on a motorway.
What is your maximum speed limit?

Mark one answer
- A. 40 mph
- B. 50 mph
- C. 60 mph
- D. 70 mph

The national speed limit for a car towing a trailer is the same for dual carriageways and motorways. For goods vehicles exceeding 7.5 tonnes maximum laden weight, the speed limit on dual carriageways is 50 mph unless a lower limit is in force.

Q340 A basic rule when driving on motorways is

Mark one answer
- A. Keep to the left lane unless overtaking
- B. Overtake on the side that is clearest
- C. Try to keep above 50 mph to prevent congestion
- D. Use the lane that has least traffic

If conditions are good and you can see well ahead you should drive at a steady speed which suits you and your vehicle. Keep a safe gap from the vehicle in front. Do not exceed the speed limit. Do not obstruct faster traffic by driving slowly in the middle or outer lane. You must not overtake on the left a vehicle moving slowly in the middle or outer lane.

Q341 **The left-hand lane on a three-lane motorway is for use by**

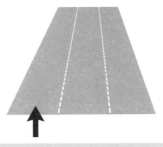

Mark one answer

- **A.** Any vehicle
- **B.** Emergency vehicles only
- **C.** Large vehicles only
- **D.** Slow vehicles only

If the left lane is occupied by a convoy of slow-moving vehicles, use the lane to the right to overtake but move back into the left lane afterwards.

Q342 **The left-hand lane of a motorway should be used for**

Mark one answer

- **A.** Breakdowns and emergencies only
- **B.** Normal driving
- **C.** Overtaking slower traffic in the other lanes
- **D.** Slow vehicles only

Do not confuse the left lane with the hard shoulder. Never drive on the hard shoulder unless you are directed to do so or you are pulling over to stop because of an emergency breakdown.

Q343 **You are driving on a three-lane motorway at 70 mph. There is no traffic ahead. Which lane should you use?**

Mark one answer

- **A.** Any lane
- **B.** Left lane
- **C.** Middle lane
- **D.** Right lane

When approaching a junction, make sure you are in the correct lane. At some junctions the left lane may take you off the motorway or on to another one.

Q344 **On a three-lane motorway, which lane should you use for normal driving?**

Mark one answer
- A. Centre
- B. Right
- C. Either the right or centre
- D. Left

Use the centre lane for overtaking slower traffic in the left lane. Make sure the centre lane is clear enough of traffic behind and ahead of you **before** you signal and change lanes to overtake.

Q345 **For what reason may you use the right-hand lane of a motorway?**

Mark one answer
- A. For driving at more than 70 mph
- B. For keeping out of the way of lorries
- C. For overtaking other vehicles
- D. For turning right

On a two-lane or three-lane motorway the left lane is for normal driving and the other lanes are for overtaking slow moving traffic. Sometimes numbers are used instead of names when referring to lanes. On a three-lane motorway the left lane is lane 1, the centre is lane 2 and the right lane is lane 3. It is **wrong** to call lane 3 the fast lane.

Q346 **On motorways you should never overtake on the left UNLESS**

Mark one answer
- A. You warn drivers behind by signalling left
- B. You can see well ahead that the hard shoulder is clear
- C. There is a queue of traffic to your right that is moving more slowly
- D. The traffic in the right-hand lane is signalling right

When you signal left (or right) on the motorway you indicate your intention to move into the lane on your left (or right). If you are already in the left lane, your left signal indicates your intention to leave the motorway. When you have changed lanes or joined the exit slipway, you should normally cancel your signal.

Q347 What colour are the reflective studs between the lanes on a motorway?

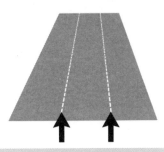

Mark one answer
- **A.** Amber
- **B.** Green
- **C.** Red
- **D.** White

The colours **red** and **amber** signify danger. Think of the traffic lights. On the motorway the red or amber cats' eyes tell you where you must **not** drive.

Q348 What colour are the reflective studs between a motorway and its slip road?

Mark one answer
- **A.** Amber
- **B.** Green
- **C.** Red
- **D.** White

Think of the traffic lights. The colour **green** indicates that you may go if your way forward is clear. On the motorway the green cats' eyes tell you where you may drive.

Q349 You are travelling on a motorway. What colour are the cats' eyes on the left of the carriageway?

Mark one answer
- **A.** Amber
- **B.** Green
- **C.** Red
- **D.** White

Remember that you must not cross from the left-hand lane in order to drive along the hard shoulder.

Q350 On a motorway the amber studs can be found between

Mark one answer
- A. Each pair of the lanes
- B. The acceleration lane and the carriageway
- C. The central reservation and the carriageway
- D. The hard shoulder and the carriageway

You must not cross, park or stop on the central reservation. You may stop on the hard shoulder but only in the event of a breakdown or real emergency.

Q351 You are driving on a three-lane motorway. There are red cats' eyes on your left and white cats' eyes to your right. Where are you?

Mark one answer
- A. In the left-hand lane
- B. In the middle lane
- C. In the right-hand lane
- D. On the hard shoulder

White reflective studs on ordinary roads, dual carriageways and motorways serve the same purpose at night as white hazard lines do during the day. They separate streams of traffic. See **Q152**, **Q433** and **Q434**.

Q352 What do these motorway signs show?

Mark one answer
- A. They are countdown markers to a bridge
- B. They are countdown markers to the next exit
- C. They are distance markers to the next telephone
- D. They warn of a police control ahead

On dual carriageways, the countdown markers to an exit are white stripes on a green background. The countdown markers to a concealed level crossing are red stripes on a white background.

Q353 You are driving on a motorway. By mistake, you go past the exit which you wanted to take. You should

Mark one answer
- A. Carefully reverse on the hard shoulder
- B. Carefully reverse in the left-hand lane
- C. Carry on to the next exit
- D. Make a U-turn at the next gap in the central reservation

Plan your journey on a motorway. Study a motorway map and write down the number of any exit you will take and the number of the one before it. Look for these numbers on the motorway information signs. Make sure you are in the correct in plenty of time to join the exit slip-way you require. If you pass your exit there is no turning back.

Q354 You are travelling in the left-hand lane of a busy motorway. Signs indicate that your lane is closed 800 yards ahead. You should

Mark one answer
- A. Move over to the lane on your right as soon as it is safe
- B. Signal right, then pull up and wait for someone to give way
- C. Switch on your hazard warning lights and edge over to the lane on your right
- D. Wait until you reach the obstruction, then move across to the right

There is always more than one sign to warn of a lane closure. It is dangerous, inconsiderate driving to leave your lane change until you reach the obstruction. Be prepared to get into position early and, if necessary, to reduce speed to allow others to change lanes. See **Q324**.

Q355 When driving through a contraflow system on a motorway you should

Mark one answer
- A. Drive close to the vehicle ahead to reduce queues
- B. Ensure you do not exceed 30mph, for safety
- C. Keep a good distance from the vehicle ahead, for safety
- D. Switch lanes to keep the traffic flowing

Contraflow systems and speed restrictions are introduced when essential repairs and roadworks are in progress. Cones are often used to separate lanes of traffic. Drive carefully and observe the restrictions. Watch out for workers and other pedestrians who are always at risk in these circumstances.

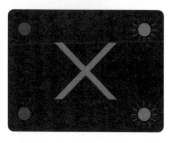

Q356 **You are driving on the motorway. There are red flashing lights above each lane. You must**

Mark one answer
- A. Leave at the next exit
- B. Pull on to the hard shoulder
- C. Slow down and watch for further signals
- D. Stop and wait

Motorway signals situated on the central reservation apply to all lanes of traffic. On an overhead gantry, separate signals apply for each individual lane. Overhead flashing red lights would be a serious hazard warning signal drivers must not ignore.

Q357 **When may you stop on a motorway?**

Mark three answers
- A. If a child in the car feels ill
- B. If red lights show above the lanes
- C. If you have to read a map
- D. In an emergency or a breakdown
- E. When told to by the police
- F. When you are tired and need a rest

Use the facilities at a motorway service area if you are tired and need a rest or a child in your car feels ill. If you are alone in the car and you need to check your route on a map, leave the motorway by the first available exit to find a safe and convenient place to stop. See **Q269** to **Q271**.

Q358 **When are you NOT allowed to stop on the motorway?**

Mark one answer
- A. To pick up something that has dropped off your vehicle
- B. To prevent an accident
- C. When the police tell you to
- D. When there are red flashing light signals above your lane

You **must stop** on the motorway when the police tell you to stop or when red lights are flashing on the central reservation, above all lanes or just above your lane. You must also stop to prevent an accident, so be prepared to stop if the vehicle up ahead has its hazard warning lights flashing. See **Q268**.

Q359 **On a motorway, you may ONLY stop on the hard shoulder**

Mark one answer
- A. If you feel tired and need to rest
- B. If you accidentally go past the exit that you wanted to take
- C. In an emergency
- D. To pick up a hitch-hiker

If your vehicle breaks down, you should stop on the extreme left of the hard shoulder then move yourself and your passengers away on to the verge. Pedestrians are not allowed on the motorway. It is an offence to pick up or set down anyone on a slip road or on any other part of the motorway.

Q360 **What should you use the hard shoulder of a motorway for?**

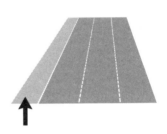

Mark one answer
- A. Joining the motorway
- B. Overtaking
- C. Stopping in an emergency
- D. Stopping when you are tired

The hard shoulder is for emergencies. You may stop on it but only in an emergency. You must never drive along it unless you are directed to do so. The hard shoulder may sometimes be the only route the police and emergency services can use to get to an accident.

Q361 **You get a puncture on the motorway. You manage to get your vehicle on to the hard shoulder. You should**

Mark one answer
- A. Change the wheel yourself immediately
- B. Only change the wheel if you have a passenger to help you
- C. Try to wave down another vehicle for help
- D. Use the emergency telephone and call for assistance

The police and emergency services need to keep the hard shoulder clear and they need to know that it is clear of any obstruction. If your vehicle breaks down on the motorway, your first duty is to warn other traffic and inform the motorway authorities immediately. See **Q273**.

Q362 **Your car has broken down on the motorway. You have stopped on the hard shoulder. Where is the safest place for you to wait for help?**

Mark one answer
- **A.** Behind the car
- **B.** In the car
- **C.** In front of the car
- **D.** On the grass bank

A stationary vehicle is at risk and a danger to other motorway users even when it is on the hard shoulder with its hazard lights flashing. You and your passengers ought to get as far from it as possible until the emergency services arrive. See **Q272**.

Q363 **You have broken down on the motorway. Your vehicle is on the hard shoulder. Your passengers should**

Mark one answer
- **A.** Leave the vehicle and wait on the embankment
- **B.** Leave the vehicle and walk to the nearest exit from the motorway
- **C.** Stay in their seats with their seat belts on
- **D.** Undo their seat belts but stay in their seats

Keep any children under control. If any passengers have to remain seated in the vehicle, they should keep their seat belt on. Only one person should walk on the hard shoulder to the nearest emergency telephone to alert the police.

Q364 **Your vehicle has broken down on a motorway. You are not able to stop on the hard shoulder. What should you do FIRST?**

Mark one answer
- **A.** Attempt to repair your vehicle quickly
- **B.** Place a warning triangle in the road
- **C.** Stop following traffic and ask for help
- **D.** Switch on your hazard warning lights

If your vehicle breaks down on the carriageway, your first priority is to warn the drivers of vehicles coming from behind you. You should stay inside your vehicle and wear your seat belt unless you can be certain of getting safely across to the verge.

Q365 **Why is it particularly important to carry out a check on your vehicle before making a long motorway journey?**

Mark one answer

○ **A.** High speeds may increase the risk of your vehicle breaking down

○ **B.** Motorway service stations do not deal with breakdowns

○ **C.** The road surface will wear down the tyres faster

○ **D.** You will have to do more harsh braking on motorways

Follow the manufacturer's recommendation when you adjust your tyre pressures for a heavily loaded car. Do not over-inflate them. It is illegal and it causes them unnecessary wear. The risk of accidents is greater if tyres are over-inflated. Remember also to make sure the tyre on your spare wheel is correctly inflated. All your tyres must meet the minimum depth of tread requirements. It would be no defence in law to claim that they had worn down during your journey. See **Q167** and **Q168**.

Q366 **What should you do when you see this sign?**

Mark one answer
- ○ **A.** Stop even if the road is clear
- ○ **B.** Stop ONLY if children are waiting to cross
- ○ **C.** Stop ONLY if a red light is showing
- ○ **D.** Stop ONLY if traffic is approaching

You must stop and give way at a junction with an unbroken white line across the road. The eight-sided shape of the road sign makes it different from all other road signs and easily identified even if there is snow on it. You must stop at and behind the line. It is an offence to drive over the line without stopping. Take extra care at these dangerous junctions.

Q367 **You MUST obey signs giving orders. These signs are mostly in**

Mark one answer
- ○ **A.** Blue rectangles
- ○ **B.** Green rectangles
- ○ **C.** Red circles
- ○ **D.** Red triangles

Signs in rectangles usually give information. An important exception is the sign for one-way traffic (white arrow on a blue rectangle). Do not confuse it with the sign for ahead only (white arrow on a blue circle). Signs in triangles usually give warning. An important exception is the sign for give way (an 'upside-down' triangle – one standing on its point).

Q368 **What does a circular traffic sign with a blue background do?**

Mark one answer
- ○ **A.** Give directions
- ○ **B.** Give an instruction
- ○ **C.** Give motorway information
- ○ **D.** Give warning of a motorway ahead

A **red** colour warns you of danger and orders you **not** to do something. A **blue** colour is used on signs giving you an order and on motorway signs giving you information.

Q369 What does this sign mean?

Mark one answer
- A. Lay-by 30 miles ahead
- B. Maximum speed 30 mph
- C. Minimum speed 30 mph
- D. Service area 30 miles ahead

The common mistake is driving too fast for the conditions. Most speed limit signs are black numbers on a white circle with a red edge. They tell you the highest speed you are allowed. They do not tell you the safest speed to drive.

Q370 What does this sign mean?

Mark one answer
- A. Clearway – no stopping
- B. National speed limit applies
- C. Waiting restrictions apply
- D. Waiting permitted

Yellow lines on the kerb and at the edge of the road indicate where loading and waiting restrictions are in force. The times when restrictions are in force are usually displayed on a nearby plate or on signs at the entry to restriction zones. The reason for the restrictions is road safety. The general rule is the more paint, the more restrictions because of the greater danger. Double yellow lines on the road with triple yellow lines on the kerb signify no loading or unloading at any time on any day in the year. Where waiting, but not loading, is restricted or prohibited, there is usually a 20-minute time limit on loading but this is not shown on the signs. Restrictions on loading and unloading include picking up and setting down passengers. See **Q428**.

Q371 You see this sign ahead. It means

Mark one answer
- A. National speed limit applies
- B. No entry
- C. No stopping
- D. Waiting restrictions apply

The **NO ENTRY** sign is a horizontal white strip on a red circle. It tells you **not** to drive over the two broken white lines marking the exit end of a one-way street. The national speed limit sign is a diagonal black strip on a white circle. See **Q383**. The sign warning you of waiting restrictions is a diagonal red line on a blue circle with a red border. See **Q370**. The word **END** on a white plate underneath a clearway sign means that stopping restrictions do not apply beyond the sign.

Q372 What does a sign with a brown background show?

Mark one answer
- A. Motorway routes
- B. Minor routes
- C. Primary roads
- D. Tourist directions

Signs for primary roads usually have a green background. Minor road signs may be black on a white background. Sometimes they have a blue border. Sometimes they are white on a blue background.

Q373 Traffic signs giving orders are generally which shape?

Mark one answer

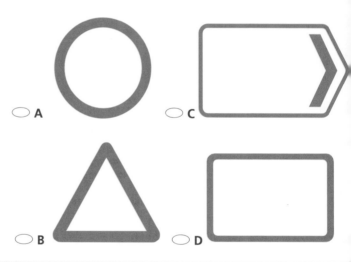

- A
- B
- C
- D

Scan the road as far ahead as possible for road signs. From the shape you will know in advance if the sign will give you an order, a warning or information. This helps you to prepare in good time for any actions required on your part.

Q374 Which type of sign tells you NOT to do something?

Mark one answer

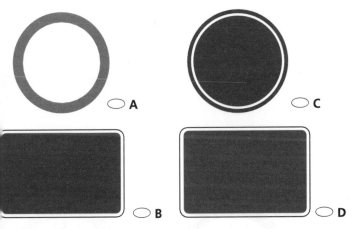

○ A   ○ C   ○ B   ○ D

Scan the road as far ahead as possible for the colour of any road signs. This will give you advance warning to prepare in good time for any negative or positive actions required on your part.

Q375 What does this sign mean?

Mark one answer
○ **A.** Do not overtake
○ **B.** Form two lanes
○ **C.** Keep in one lane
○ **D.** Priority to traffic coming towards you

Remember a **circle** means **must** and **red** means **not**. Avoid confusing this sign with the sign on a **rectangle** giving you **information** about your priority and oncoming vehicles. See **Q380** and **Q381**.

Q376 What does this sign mean?

Mark one answer
○ **A.** No motor vehicles
○ **B.** No overtaking
○ **C.** Two-way traffic
○ **D.** You have priority

Two black arrows on a white triangle with a red border warns you of two-way traffic. See **Q380**, **Q381** and **Q387**.

Q377 What does this sign mean?

Mark one answer
- A. Do not overtake
- B. No right turn ahead
- C. Oncoming cars have priority
- D. Two-way traffic

Oncoming vehicles can only have priority if you give it to them. The sign ordering you to give priority to oncoming vehicles is on a white circle with a red border. See **Q379**. The **red** arrow means you **must not** take priority.

Q378 Which sign means no overtaking?

Mark one answer

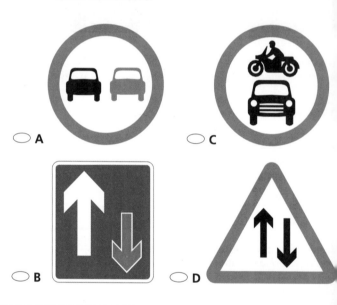

A

C

B

D

Even when overtaking is allowed, always ask yourself if you really need to overtake. If you are going to overtake, make sure it is safe and do follow the **P-S-L-M-S-M** routine. See **Q210** to **Q212**.

Q379 What does this traffic sign mean?

Mark one answer
- A. Give priority to oncoming traffic
- B. No overtaking allowed
- C. No U-turns allowed
- D. One-way traffic only

Remember a **circle** means **must** and **red** means **not**. The **red** arrow means you **must not** take priority over oncoming vehicles.

Q380 What does this sign mean?

Mark one answer
- A. No overtaking
- B. Two-way traffic ahead
- C. You have priority over vehicles from the opposite direction
- D. You are entering a one-way street

Remember that **rectangle** usually means **information**. You have priority only when another driver gives it to you. Take care in case the drivers of oncoming vehicles ignore the sign ordering them to give you priority.

Q381 What is the meaning of this traffic sign?

Mark one answer
- A. Bus lane ahead
- B. End of two-way road
- C. Give priority to vehicles coming towards you
- D. You have priority over vehicles coming towards you

Remember **red** means **not**. The **red** arrow means oncoming traffic ought **not** to take priority over you. Proceed carefully just in case they do.

Q382 Which sign means NO motor vehicles allowed?

Mark one answer

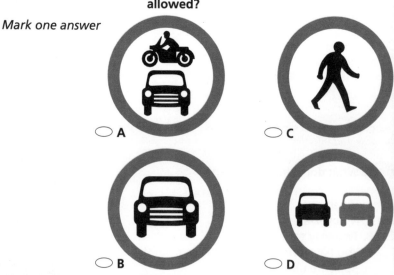

○ A

○ C

○ B

○ D

If the sign shows a car on its own, then solo motorcycles, scooters and mopeds are allowed entry but a motorcycle with a side-car attached is not allowed. When the sign is just an empty white circle with a red border, even cycles are not permitted. See **Q383**.

Q383 Which sign means NO vehicles are allowed?

Mark one answer

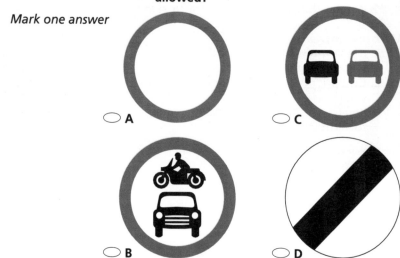

○ A

○ C

○ B

○ D

Always look at any plate beneath a sign restricting entry to a road. Sometimes certain vehicles may be allowed entry to the road for access only. In the eyes of the law, pushing a cycle is not different from riding it. Strictly speaking, you should never push a cycle over a pedestrian crossing. You should carry it. The law then regards it as a parcel.

Q384 **What does this sign mean?**

Mark one answer
- **A.** Cars and motorcycles only
- **B.** Clearway – no stopping
- **C.** No motor vehicles
- **D.** No overtaking

A motor vehicle is a vehicle powered by an engine and capable of transporting one or more people. Cars and motorcycles are not the only motor vehicles. Buses, coaches, mopeds, tractors and other vehicles are included.

Q385 **What are triangular signs for?**

Mark one answer
- **A.** To give directions
- **B.** To give information
- **C.** To give orders
- **D.** To give warnings

Apart from the 'upside-down' **GIVE WAY** triangle, you do not have to obey signs in triangles. But if you ignore any of these warning signs you do so at your peril. Many, if not most, give you advance warning of hazards ahead that are temporarily hidden from your view.

Q386 **What does this traffic sign mean?**

Mark one answer
- **A.** Danger ahead
- **B.** Service area ahead
- **C.** Slippery road ahead
- **D.** Tyres liable to punctures ahead

Triangular signs warn you of specific hazards. The sign warning you of danger ahead may have a plate underneath to indicate the nature of the danger: e.g. **FALLEN TREE, HIDDEN DIP,** etc. Be sure to read any plate fixed underneath a road sign.

Q387 What does this sign mean?

Mark one answer
- A. Motorway contraflow system ahead
- B. Traffic approaching you has priority
- C. Two-way traffic straight ahead
- D. Two-way traffic ahead across a one-way street

Signs warning of changing traffic flow are very important. A pair of oppositely-facing arrows means vehicles travelling in opposite directions. If the pair of arrows is horizontal, the sign means two-way traffic ahead and across a one-way street.

Q388 Which of these signs means there is a series of bends ahead?

Mark one answer

Good drivers use warning signs to plan their approach to a bend. The sign tells you whether you are approaching a single bend or a series of bends. It also tells you whether the single bend is a left-hand or a right-hand bend. For a series of bends, the sign tells you whether the first bend is a left-hand or a right-hand one. Black and white chevrons are often used as well if the bends are particularly sharp or dangerous.

Q389 **Which of these signs warns you of a pedestrian crossing?**

Mark one answer

A

C

B

D

Always take notice of warning signs showing pedestrians, especially if they depict children or the elderly. Pay special attention to your road position and speed when the sign warns that pedestrians may be walking on the road itself.

Q390 **What does this sign mean?**

Mark one answer

- **A.** No pedestrians allowed
- **B.** Pedestrian crossing ahead
- **C.** Pedestrian zone – no vehicles
- **D.** School crossing patrol

Remember a **circle** means **must** and **red** means **not**. A picture of a pedestrian on a white circle with a red border means no pedestrians are allowed. You should still watch out for pedestrians even when you pass a 'no pedestrians' sign. A picture of children on a white triangle with a red border may have a **SCHOOL** plate underneath. A **PATROL** plate tells you to be prepared to stop when you see the **STOP–CHILDREN** sign being held up. See **Q52** to **Q56**.

Q391 What does this sign mean?

Mark one answer
- A. No footpath ahead
- B. Pedestrian crossing ahead
- C. Pedestrians only ahead
- D. School crossing ahead

Approach any crossing with care. Be prepared to reduce speed. Remember that a pedestrian becomes entitled to absolute priority just by placing one foot on a zebra crossing. Make eye contact with the pedestrians, give them a proper arm signal to show you are stopping, but never wave them on to the crossing. See **Q14**.

Q392 What does this sign mean?

Mark one answer
- A. Bicycles are not allowed
- B. Cyclists must dismount
- C. Walking is not allowed
- D. You are approaching a cycle route

Remember that signs giving **orders** are usually **circles**. Signs giving **information** are usually **rectangles**.

Q393 What does this sign mean?

Mark one answer
- A. Adverse camber
- B. Airport
- C. Crosswinds
- D. Road noise

You often see signs with a picture of a flying aircraft in the vicinity of signs with a picture of a windsock. Airports are in large, flat open areas where strong gusting winds may cause problems for aircraft on the runways and for two-wheeled or high-sided traffic on nearby roads.

Q394 Which FOUR of these would be indicated by a triangular road sign?

Mark four answers
- A. Ahead only
- B. Children crossing
- C. Low bridge
- D. Minimum speed
- E. Road narrows
- F. T-junction

Remember that signs on **blue circles** give **positive instructions** you **must obey**. Signs on triangles give warnings you may ignore at your peril. See **Q368**.

Q395 What does this sign mean?

Mark one answer
- A. Railway station
- B. Ring road
- C. Route for cyclists
- D. Scenic route

A white picture of a cycle on a blue background indicates a cycle route. The sign may be on a circle or a rectangle. Direction signs for a railway station have a distinctive white symbol on a solid red rectangle.

Q396 What does this sign mean?

Mark one answer
- A. Rest area
- B. Ring road
- C. Roundabout
- D. Route for lorries

A white **H** on a solid blue rectangle is the sign for hospital. A black **HR** on a solid yellow rectangle is the sign for a holiday route.

Q397 What does this sign mean?

Mark one answer
- **A.** End of bus lane
- **B.** End of motorway
- **C.** No motor vehicles
- **D.** No through road

A red diagonal line may cancel a sign: no left turn, no right turn, no U-turn, traffic lights not working, end of minimum speed, etc. Do not confuse these signs with those for clearway and for parking restrictions. See **Q370**, **Q371** and **Q413**.

Q398 What does this sign mean?

Mark one answer
- **A.** Right-hand lane for buses only
- **B.** No turning to the right
- **C.** The right-hand lane is closed
- **D.** The right-hand lane ahead is narrow

The number and position of the arrows and red bars will vary according to which lanes are temporarily open or closed. A horizontal red bar at the top of a vertical white bar on a solid blue rectangle is the sign for a permanent 'no through road'.

Q399 What does this motorway sign mean?

Mark one answer
- **A.** No services for 50 miles
- **B.** Obstruction 50 metres ahead
- **C.** Temporary maximum speed 50 mph
- **D.** Temporary minimum speed 50 mph

On urban motorways, overhead gantries can carry matrix light signs for each individual lane. On rural motorways the signs are fixed in the central reservations and apply to the traffic in all lanes. These signs are normally two miles apart. These matrix light signs are designed to give temporary and changing signals. If you ignore any advisory signs, you may not commit an offence but you may lose favour in a court of law. Take notice of these signs even if the reasons for them are not immediately obvious.

Q400 What does this motorway sign mean?

Mark one answer
- **A.** Change to the lane on your left
- **B.** Change to the opposite carriageway
- **C.** Leave the motorway at the next exit
- **D.** Pull up on the hard shoulder

The motorway matrix light sign instructing you to leave the motorway at the next exit is an arrow bent upwards and pointing to the left. You must not confuse it with the sign telling you to change lanes.

Q401 On a motorway this sign means

Mark one answer
- **A.** Leave the motorway at the next exit
- **B.** Move to the lane on your left
- **C.** Move over on to the hard shoulder
- **D.** Pass a temporary obstruction on the left

A sign telling you to change lanes might instruct you to move into the lane on your right or your left. Note which way the arrow is pointing. And don't forget your mirror and signal before you change lanes. Move as soon as possible but only when it is safe.

Q402 What does this sign mean?

Mark one answer
- **A.** Right-hand lane closed ahead
- **B.** Right-hand lane T-junction only
- **C.** Through traffic use left lane
- **D.** 11-ton weight limit

This is a typical matrix light sign used on some motorways and dual carriageways to warn drivers of danger or problems up ahead. See **Q398**.

Q403 **You are driving on a motorway. Red flashing lights appear above your lane. What should you do?**

Mark one answer
- A. Continue in that lane and await further information
- B. Drive on to the hard shoulder
- C. Go no further in that lane
- D. Stop and wait for an instruction to proceed

You must never ignore flashing red lights. They always mean danger. Remember that at railway crossings the flashing red lights mean that you must stop because trains are approaching. Matrix light signs do not issue further instructions but they do provide warnings on weather and road conditions ahead.

Q404 **A red traffic light means**

Mark one answer
- A. Proceed with caution
- B. Stop if you are able to brake safely
- C. You must stop and wait behind the stop line
- D. You should stop unless turning left

An illuminated red traffic light has only one meaning. It is extremely dangerous and a very serious offence to ignore it. Remember that even when the traffic lights show green you must not go unless it is safe and your way forward is clear.

Q405 **A red traffic light means**

Mark one answer
- A. You may drive straight on if there is no other traffic
- B. You may turn left if it is safe to do so
- C. You must slow down and prepare to stop if traffic has started to cross
- D. You must stop behind the white stop line

Make sure you know the sequence of traffic light signals. If you plan your driving carefully you can often arrive at a junction when the traffic lights are showing green. Remember that you can tell from a distance whether they are traffic lights or pelican crossing lights by the amber light. The traffic light is a steady amber following the red light. The pelican crossing light flashes amber before the green light shows.

Q406 You are approaching a red traffic light.
The signal will change from red to

Mark one answer
- **A.** Amber then green
- **B.** Green then amber
- **C.** Green and amber then green
- **D.** Red and amber then green

At a pelican crossing when the red light changes to flashing amber, vehicles may proceed if the crossing is clear or any pedestrians are out of danger.

Q407 You are approaching traffic lights. Red and
amber are showing. This means

Mark one answer
- **A.** Pass the lights if the road is clear
- **B.** There is a fault with the lights – take care
- **C.** The lights are about to change to red
- **D.** Wait for the green light before you pass
the lights

Only a green traffic light means you may go but even then you must be sure that it is safe to proceed. Remember to watch out for traffic 'jumping the lights'. Listen as well as look for the possibility of police vehicles, ambulances and other vehicles driving through the traffic lights to an emergency.

Q408 You are at a junction controlled by traffic
lights. When should you NOT proceed at
green?

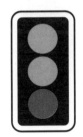

Mark one answer
- **A.** When pedestrians are waiting to cross
- **B.** When your exit from the junction is
blocked
- **C.** When you intend to turn right
- **D.** When you think the lights may be about to
change

You give priority to pedestrians when they are on a crossing or in danger on the road. Remember also the general road that you should not proceed unless it is safe and your way forward is clear.

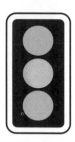

Q409 **At traffic lights, amber on its own means**

Mark one answer
- A. Prepare to go
- B. Go if the way is clear
- C. Go if no pedestrians are crossing
- D. Stop at the stop line

At traffic lights the steady amber light on its own will always be followed by the red light. You may go against the amber light if it comes on after you have crossed the stop line. You should plan your approach and arrive at a sensible speed. But if you are so close to the line that you might cause an accident by pulling up, you may go against the amber. Bear in mind the possibility of crossing traffic moving off when red and amber are still showing together.

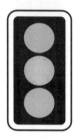

Q410 **You see this traffic light ahead. Which light(s) will come on next?**

Mark one answer
- A. Green alone
- B. Green and amber together
- C. Red alone
- D. Red and amber together

Green and amber lights at traffic signals never show at the same time. When red and amber show together you can prepare to move off when they have changed and your way forward is safe and clear.

Q411 You are in the left hand lane at traffic lights. You are waiting to turn left. At which of these traffic lights must you NOT move on?

Mark one answer

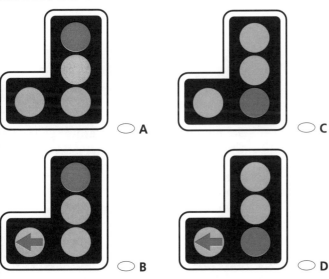

○ A

○ C

○ B

○ D

When you are waiting at a junction, study the arrangement and operation of the traffic lights. You may see an arrow on the green light to indicate the direction you must follow. You may also see extra green lights with arrows to control traffic filtering left or right at the junction. When there is more than one set of lights, make sure you understand which ones apply to you.

Q412 A pelican crossing shows the flashing green man signal. What signal do drivers see?

Mark one answer
○ **A.** Red
○ **B.** Red and amber
○ **C.** Flashing amber
○ **D.** Flashing green

The green light seen by drivers never flashes. Red and amber show together at traffic lights but not at pelican crossings. When the green man starts flashing, pedestrians must not start to cross but those already on the crossing should continue. See **Q104, Q105.**

Q413 What does this sign mean?

Mark one answer
- **A.** Amber signal out of order
- **B.** New traffic lights ahead
- **C.** Temporary traffic lights ahead
- **D.** Traffic lights out of order

Remember that a red diagonal line may cancel a sign: end of motorway, no left turn, no right turn, no U-turn, etc. Do not confuse this with the diagonal of the sign warning of parking restrictions in force. See **Q397**.

Q414 You approach a junction. The traffic lights are not working. A police officer gives this signal. You should

Mark one answer
- **A.** Stop at the stop line
- **B.** Stop level with the officer's arm
- **C.** Turn left only
- **D.** Turn right only

Police officers or traffic wardens will raise and move their arm as a signal for you to move. They will hold up but not move their arm as a signal for you to stop. Their arm is vertical for traffic in front of them and horizontal for traffic behind them.

Q415 Which THREE are legally authorised to direct traffic?

Mark three answers
- **A.** Anyone assisting the driver of a large vehicle to reverse
- **B.** A farm worker in charge of livestock crossing the road
- **C.** A road-worker operating a stop-go board
- **D.** A school crossing warden
- **E.** A teacher in charge of children who are crossing the road
- **F.** A traffic warden

A little courtesy and consideration can mean a great deal to other road users. Controlling a group of children outside the classroom can sometimes tax the patience of the best teacher. Directing a herd of animals along a road usually requires two people and is never easy. And manoeuvring a large vehicle can be difficult and dangerous without somebody at the back to guide you.

Q416 There is a police car following you. The police officer flashes the headlights and points to the left. What should you do?

Mark one answer
- A. Move over to the left
- B. Pull up on the left
- C. Stop immediately
- D. Turn next left

Uniformed police officers have the authority to stop anyone at any time. In the interests of safety, officers in a police car will normally stop a motorist. To attract a motorist's attention, the officer may flash the headlights or the blue light and/or sound the siren. To signal to the motorist to pull over, the officer may point to the left and switch on the left indicator. It is an offence not to stop when directed. But if for some reason you feel threatened or in danger, you should aim for the nearest police station or public place before actually stopping.

Q417 How will a police officer in a patrol vehicle get you to stop?

Mark one answer
- A. Flash the headlights, indicate left and point to the left
- B. Pull alongside you, use the siren and wave you to stop
- C. Use the siren, overtake then cut in front and stop
- D. Wait until you stop then approach you

Police drivers normally use the siren and flashing blue lights in an emergency to warn other road users. They could be hurrying to the scene of an accident. The flashing blue light indicates that you should give the police car priority. Slow down and move over to make way for them and any emergency services following them. When escorting vehicles with wide loads, police normally use only flashing blue lights and headlights to warn traffic.

Q418 When motorists flash their headlights at you it means

Mark one answer
- A. They are giving way to you
- B. There is a radar speed trap ahead
- C. There is something wrong with your vehicle
- D. They are warning you of their presence

You will confuse and endanger other road users by flashing your headlights unless you are drawing their attention to your presence because there is threat of danger from another moving vehicle. It is an offence to warn other motorists of a speed trap. See **Q95**, **Q113** to **Q115** and **Q124**.

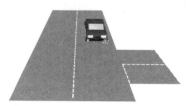

Q419 You are waiting at a T-junction. A vehicle is coming from the right with the left signal flashing. What should you do?

Mark one answer
- A. Move out and accelerate hard
- B. Move out slowly
- C. Pull out before the vehicle reaches the junction
- D. Wait until the vehicle starts to turn in

Flashing headlights, flashing hazard lights and a flashing indicator all warn you of a vehicle's presence. The headlights tell you nothing else. Hazard lights warn you of danger. A flashing indicator may or may not be a signal of the driver's intention to change speed and or direction. Drivers can and do occasionally forget to cancel an unwanted signal.

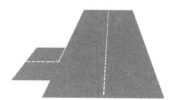

Q420 You want to stop just after a side road to the left. How should you signal?

Mark one answer
- A. Give no signal at all
- B. Give a slowing down arm signal before the junction
- C. Signal left before the junction
- D. Wait until you have passed the junction, then signal left

Good drivers know how and when to give a signal. Always aim to give other road users the clearest and earliest indication of your intentions. Remember that when you move the arm of your indicator switch there is always a slight delay before your signal lights actually start flashing. See **Q2**.

Q421 You want to turn right at a junction, but you think that your indicators cannot be seen clearly. What should you do?

Mark one answer
- A. Get out and check if your indicators can be seen
- B. Give an arm signal as well as an indicator signal
- C. Keep well over to the right
- D. Stay in the left hand lane

You keep to the left when you are going to turn left at a junction. Sometimes you keep to the left when you are going to turn right because you are allowing for large vehicles turning into the road or because the road is narrow. Always consider the possibility of giving a proper arm signal especially at pedestrian crossings.

Q422 How should you give an arm signal to turn LEFT?

Mark one answer

○ A   ○ B   ○ C   ○ D

Use only the arm signals shown in The Highway Code. Give the signal properly and in good time. Try to make eye contact with the other road users but do **not** wave to other them. Think **arm (not hand)** signal.

Q423 Which arm signal tells a following vehicle you intend to turn left?

Mark one answer

○ A   ○ B   ○ C   ○ D

The arm signal you give for turning right is the same whether it is to a person controlling traffic or to other road users. This is not true for your signal to turn left. Remember that you use only your right arm to signal to traffic behind you.

Q424 When may you sound the horn on your vehicle?

Mark one answer
- ○ A. To attract a friend's attention
- ○ B. To give you right of way
- ○ C. To make slower drivers move over
- ○ D. To warn other drivers of your presence

Revise these questions: Q58 to Q62, Q64, Q74, Q86, Q90 and Q91, Q97, Q103, Q112 and Q113, Q124, Q130, Q133, Q145, Q182, Q201 and Q202.

Q425 At this junction there is a stop sign with a solid white line on the road surface. Why?

Mark one answer
- A. It is a busy junction
- B. Speed on the major road is de-restricted
- C. There are hazard warning lines in the centre of the road
- D. Visibility along the major road is restricted

When you see the eight-sided **STOP** up ahead, you know that you **must stop** at the line when you reach the junction. Do not stop back from the line. Never commit the offence of driving over the line before stopping. After you have stopped, you may then have to inch your way forward in order to check that is is safe to proceed. You must always give way to traffic on the major road.

Q426 You see this line across the road at a roundabout. What does it mean?

Mark one answer
- A. Give way to traffic from the right
- B. Stop at the line
- C. Traffic from the left has right of way
- D. You have right of way

In general, the junctions at roundabouts are designed to keep traffic flowing freely. On mini-roundabouts the junctions are marked with a broken white line. At larger roundabouts and other circular one-way systems you may find a junction controlled by traffic lights and the road marked with an unbroken white line.

Q427 A white line like this along the centre of the road is a

Mark one answer
- A. Bus lane marking
- B. Give way marking
- C. Hazard warning
- D. Lane marking

White lines along the middle of the road are meant to separate the traffic. They are are a warning of additional danger. You should not straddle or cross a single broken line, with long markings and short gaps, unless you can see that the road is clear well ahead. You **must not** cross a double solid white line except in an emergency. It marks an extremely dangerous section of road. Very often these hazard lines are confirmed by reflecting studs which show up in your headlight beam at night.

Q428 Which is a HAZARD WARNING line?

Mark one answer

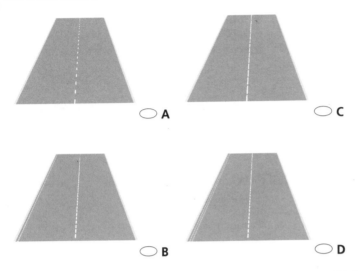

○ A

○ C

○ B

○ D

Do not confuse white lane markings with hazard warning lines. Lane markings are meant to separate streams of traffic travelling in the same direction. Hazard warning lines are meant to separate streams of traffic travelling in the opposite direction.

Q429 What does this road marking mean?

Mark one answer

○ **A.** Do not cross the line
○ **B.** No overtaking allowed
○ **C.** No stopping allowed
○ **D.** You are approaching a hazard

Broken white lines warn you of danger. A broken white line across a road warns you to give way to traffic on the major road. A broken white line along the middle of a road warns you to keep clear of traffic coming towards you on the other side of the road.

Q430 These markings mean you are approaching

Mark one answer
- A. A box junction
- B. A bus stop
- C. A parking zone
- D. A pedestrian crossing

Pedestrians should not cross the area of road bounded by white zigzag lines. You must not park on this part of the road. And you must not stop there to pick up or set down even a disabled person. Remember it is dangerous and an offence to overtake another vehicle between the zigzag lines. See **Q14, Q98**.

Q431 What do these zigzag lines at pedestrian crossings mean?

Mark one answer
- A. No parking at any time
- B. Parking allowed only for a short time
- C. Slow down to 20 mph
- D. Sounding horns is not allowed

Revise these questions: **Q15, Q16, Q98, Q99, Q294** and **Q295**.

Q432 When may you NOT overtake on the left?

Mark one answer
- A. On a free-flowing motorway or dual carriageway
- B. On a one-way street
- C. When the car in front is signalling to turn right
- D. When the traffic is moving slowly in queues

Revise these questions: **Q72, Q131, Q206, Q207, Q307,** and **Q346**.

Q433 **Where can you find amber studs on a motorway?**

Mark one answer

A. On the left hand edge of the road
B. On the right hand edge of the road
C. Separating the lanes
D. Separating the slip road from the motorway

Revise these questions: **Q347** to **Q351**.

Q434 **Where on a motorway would you find green reflective studs?**

Mark one answer

A. At slip road entrances and exits
B. Between the carriageway and the central reservation
C. Between the hard shoulder and the carriageway
D. Separating driving lanes

	2 B	3 C	4 B	5 C	6 A	7 D	8 B	9 D

HAZARD AWARENESS

10 ADE	11 AB	12 C	13 A	14 C	15 B	16 C	17 A
18 C	19 A	20 B	21 C	22 A	23 C	24 A	25 C
26 A	27 D	28 D	29 BDE	30 CD	31 ACD	32 D	33 A
34 A	35 C	36 A	37 C	38 B	39 D	40 B	41 AC
42 D	43 B	44 C	45 ACD	46 ADE	47 DEF	48 C	49 C
50 B	51 C						

VULNERABLE ROAD USERS

52 D	53 B	54 A	55 B	56 B	57 B	58 C	59 C
60 D	61 B	62 B	63 A	64 D	65 A	66 B	67 A
68 A	69 D	70 B	71 B	72 A	73 D	74 B	75 C
76 D	77 AB	78 A	79 B	80 C	81 A	82 B	83 B
84 A	85 A	86 B	87 C	88 B	89 D	90 C	91 ABD
92 A	93 D	94 A	95 D	96 D	97 C	98 CD	99 C
100 C	101 ABD						

ATTITUDE

102 B	103 A	104 B	105 B	106 C	107 B	108 A	109 D
110 C	111 D	112 A	113 C	114 A	115 B	116 D	117 C
118 B	119 AB	120 B	121 A	122 C	123 B	124 C	125 A

SECTION 2

VEHICLE HANDLING

126 C	127 C	128 D	129 AEF	130 B	131 ADE	132 C	133 B
134 D	135 AB	136 ADE	137 B	138 C	139 C	140 A	141 A
142 C	143 D	144 D	145 AB	146 B	147 C	148 D	149 A
150 A	151 C	152 C	153 A	154 C	155 C	156 C	157 BD
158 A	159 D	160 D	161 D				

VEHICLE LOADING

162 ACD	163 C	164 B	165 C	166 A	167 D	168 A	169 B
170 C	171 B						

SAFETY AND YOUR VEHICLE

172 B	173 C	174 C	175 C	176 C	177 B	178 AD	179 BEF
180 C	181 CDE	182 ACEF	183 C	184 A	185 D	186 C	187 A
188 C	189 C	190 C	191 A	192 D	193 D	194 A	195 D
196 B	197 AD	198 C	199 B	200 C	201 D	202 D	

SECTION 3

OTHER TYPES OF VEHICLE

203 A	204 C	205 D	206 B	207 A	208 B	209 B	210 D
211 C	212 D	213 A	214 B	215 A	216 D	217 A	218 ADE
219 A							

SAFETY MARGINS

220 D	221 B	222 A	223 C	224 BCE	225 C	226 C	227 AB
228 B	229 C	230 D	231 A	232 B	233 B	234 C	235 B
236 C	237 D	238 C	239 C	240 A	241 B	242 D	243 D
244 A	245 D	246 C	247 C	248 B	249 C	250 B	251 BCF
252 A							

ACCIDENTS

253 BC	254 A	255 B	256 CDE	257 ABD	258 ACDE	259 C	260 A
261 B	262 D	263 C	264 A	265 C	266 D	267 AC	268 ABD
269 D	270 C	271 B	272 D	273 B	274 BC	275 CE	276 D
277 B	278 A	279 ABC					

SECTION 4

DOCUMENTS

280 C	281 C	282 ADE	283 C	284 D	285 CE	286 B	287 C
288 B	289 BCD	290 D	291 AD				

RULES OF THE ROAD

292 AE	293 ABE	294 ABDF	295 D	296 C	297 A	298 D	299 C
300 C	301 B	302 B	303 C	304 ABD	305 C	306 BDF	307 A
308 A	309 B	310 C	311 A	312 C	313 A	314 B	315 ADE
316 CDE	317 A	318 C	319 B	320 A	321 C	322 D	323 D
324 C	325 EF	326 B	327 D	328 CE	329 B	330 A	331 A

MOTORWAY RULES

332 D	333 ACDE	334 A	335 C	336 A	337 B	338 D	339 C
340 A	341 A	342 B	343 B	344 D	345 C	346 C	347 D
348 B	349 C	350 C	351 A	352 B	353 C	354 A	355 C
356 D	357 BDE	358 A	359 C	360 C	361 D	362 D	363 A
364 D	365 A						

ROAD AND TRAFFIC SIGNS

366 A	367 C	368 B	369 C	370 C	371 C	372 D	373 A
374 A	375 A	376 B	377 A	378 A	379 A	380 C	381 D
382 A	383 A	384 C	385 D	386 A	387 C	388 A	389 A
390 B	391 B	392 D	393 C	394 BCEF	395 B	396 B	397 B
398 C	399 C	400 A	401 B	402 A	403 C	404 C	405 D
406 D	407 D	408 B	409 D	410 C	411 A	412 C	413 D
414 A	415 CDF	416 B	417 A	418 D	419 D	420 D	421 B
422 A	423 A	424 D	425 D	426 A	427 C	428 A	429 D
430 D	431 A	432 A	433 B	434 A			

AA The Driving School

SAVE £24

ON A COURSE OF 12 PREPAID LESSONS.
CALL FREE ON
0800 60 70 80

GREAT ROAD ATLASES FROM THE AA........

GLOVEBOX ATLAS BRITAIN

A fully updated edition of this highly popular pocket atlas, with the additional feature of the town plans included.

- ✻ Small handy A5 format, clear concise mapping
- ✻ 8 miles to 1 inch scale (Ireland 16 miles to 1 inch)
- ✻ AA shops and appointed garages highlighted
- ✻ 103 townplans and 10 airport plans
- ✻ Colour maps
- ✻ Index with over 4,500 place-names
- ✻ Contents listed numerically, as well as being shown on a key map
- ✻ All maps show the AA recommended through routes, one-way streets and restricted access
- ✻ Buildings of interest indicated

AA BIG ROAD ATLAS BRITAIN

The AA's best-selling atlas

❀ Fully updated with over 3,000 revisions

❀ Mapping includes new county boundaries

❀ New stand-alone town plan section, with 75 town plans including London, Dublin and Belfast

❀ Re-designed index section with over 23,000 place-names

❀ Voted Britain's clearest mapping – over 1 million copies sold since 1992

❀ Clear 3 miles to 1 inch scale, Ireland at 16 miles to 1 inch

❀ Highlighted primary route destinations

❀ Essential driving information including route-planning tips and mileage charts

❀ Greater and Central London mapping

❀ Selection of restricted motorway junctions diagrammatically represented

❀ Over 400 roadside restaurants are shown

AA GREAT BRITAIN ROAD ATLAS

The AA's best-selling hardback road atlas

- Fully updated with over 3,000 revisions
- Shows new county boundaries
- 79 town plans including London, Belfast and Dublin
- Port and airport plans
- Comprehensive 32,000 place-name index
- Voted Britain's clearest mapping
- Clear 3 miles to 1 inch mapping, Ireland at 16 miles to 1 inch
- Journey planning information, including mileage charts, AA road watch information, road signs plus a route-planning section
- Channel Tunnel feature with terminal plans of Dover & Calais
- London mapping includes a district map, 11 pages of fully indexed central London street plans, plus a map of the M25

AA MAXI SCALE ATLAS BRITAIN

The giant 2.4 miles to 1 inch scale provides the clearest ever mapping in a road atlas.

- Fully updated with over 3,000 revisions
- Shows new county boundaries
- Easy-to-see large scale, 2.4 miles to 1 inch
- Over 3/4 million copies sold since 1991
- Voted Britain's clearest mapping
- Comprehensive 32,000 place-name index
- Clear route-planning map with journey planning tips
- Motorways, primary routes, A and B roads are all clearly marked; primary route destinations are highlighted
- Useful section on using the atlas with clear explanations of symbols used
- Fully indexed map of Ireland - scale 16 miles to 1 inch
- Road map of Greater London